THE

BIRTH

OF AN EXCITING VISION

A STUDY OF **ACTS** 1:1 – 9:43

BIBLE STUDY GUIDE

From the Bible-teaching ministry of

Charles R. Swindoll

INSIGHT FOR LIVING

Charles R. Swindoll is a graduate of Dallas Theological Seminary and has served as senior pastor of the First Evangelical Free Church of Fullerton, California, since 1971. Chuck's radio program, "Insight for Living," began in 1979. In addition to his church and radio ministries, Chuck enjoys writing. He has authored numerous books and booklets on a variety of subjects.

Based on the outlines and transcripts of Chuck's sermons, the study guide text is co-authored by Bryce Klabunde, a graduate of Biola University and Dallas Theological Seminary. He also wrote the Living Insights sections.

Editor in Chief:
Cynthia Swindoll

Director, Communications Division:
Deedee Snyder

Coauthor of Text:
Bryce Klabunde

Project Manager:
Alene Cooper

Assistant Editor:
Karene Wells

Project Supervisor:
Susan Nelson

Copy Editors:
Deborah Gibbs,
Glenda Schlahta

Project Assistants:
Ellen Galey,
Cheryl Gilmore

Designer:
Gary Lett

Print Production Manager:
John Norton

Publishing System Specialist:
Bob Haskins

Printer:
Sinclair Printing Company

Unless otherwise identified, all Scripture references are from the New American Standard Bible, © The Lockman Foundation 1960, 1962, 1963, 1968, 1971, 1972, 1973, 1975, 1977. Used by permission. Scripture taken from the Holy Bible, New International Version, © 1973, 1978, 1984 International Bible Society, used by permission of Zondervan Bible Publishers. The other translation cited is the King James Version of the Bible [KJV].

An effort has been made to locate sources and obtain permission where necessary for the quotations used in this book. In the event of any unintentional omission, a modification will gladly be incorporated in future printings.

ISBN 0-8499-8439-4
Printed in the United States of America.

COVER DESIGN: Jerry Ford
COVER PHOTOGRAPH: SuperStock, Inc.
TEXT ILLUSTRATIONS (chapters 9 and 17): David Riley and Associates

CONTENTS

INTRODUCTION

We embark today on a journey that is like no other journey in the Scriptures. As we begin, a handful of frightened Christians are alone in a room, unsure of their future and unaware of how Jesus' promise would be fulfilled. By the time this journey has run its course, many of those same believers will have been transformed into models of raw courage and invincible faith. The difference, as we shall learn, was the coming and empowering of the Holy Spirit. The church was not only born, it began to impact the world in ways nobody would have imagined. In spite of severe persecution and brutal periods of martyrdom, a godly remnant continued to stand fast in determination and spread the message of the gospel of Christ to regions beyond, exactly as the risen Christ commanded.

As we get underway in our study of the book of Acts, this first volume will take us through chapter 9 . . . from the leadership of Peter to the conversion of Saul of Tarsus. The scenes are both disturbing and exciting as we witness everything from the Spirit's arrival at Pentecost to the persecution of the apostles, from the horrible stoning of Stephen to the remarkable change in Saul en route to Damascus. So hold on tight! We're in for one unforgettable journey.

Chuck Swindoll

Chuck Swindoll

PUTTING TRUTH
INTO ACTION

Knowledge apart from application falls short of God's desire for His children. He wants us to apply what we learn so that we will change and grow. This study guide was prepared with these goals in mind. As you go through the following pages, we hope your desire to discover biblical truth will grow as your understanding of God's Word increases, and that you will be encouraged to apply what you've learned.

To assist you in your study, we've included a section called ☀ **Living Insights** at the end of each lesson. These exercises will challenge you to study further and to think of specific ways to put your discoveries into action.

On occasion a lesson is followed by a ⬟**Digging Deeper** section, which gives you additional information and resources to probe further into some issues raised in that lesson.

There are many ways to use this guide—in personal devotions, group studies, discussions with friends and family, and Sunday school classes. And, of course, it's an ideal study aid when you're listening to its corresponding "Insight for Living" radio series.

To benefit most from this study guide, we would encourage you to consider it a spiritual journal. That's why we've included space in the **Living Insights** for recording your thoughts and discoveries. We hope you'll return to those sections often for review and encouragement as you continue to grow in your walk with Christ.

Bryce Klabunde

Bryce Klabunde
Coauthor of Text
Author of Living Insights

THE
BIRTH
OF AN EXCITING VISION
A STUDY OF **ACTS** 1:1 – 9:43

ACTS: THE SPREADING FLAME

Writer: Dr. Luke
Theme: The growth of the early church
Key Verse: Acts 1:8
Major People: Peter and Paul
Central Locations: Jerusalem and Antioch
Prediction Fulfilled: "I will build my church. . . ." (Matt. 16:18)

A Book of Origins:
- Coming of the Holy Spirit
- Beginning of the church and the gifts of the Spirit
- Apostolic authority
- Outbreak of persecution/martyrdom
- World missions
- Grace instead of Law

	The Church Established at Jerusalem*	The Church Scattered to Judea and Samaria*	The Church Extended to "Remotest Part"*
	The church is . . .	The gospel is . . .	The witness is . . .
	. . . born	. . . spreading	. . . extended
	. . . tested	. . . multiplying	. . . received and rejected
	. . . purified	. . . changing lives	. . . unifying Jews and Gentiles
	. . . strengthened	. . . breaking traditions	
Chapter Numbers	A.D. 30 1 — 7	8 — 12	13 — 28 A.D. 60
Leaders	The Apostle Peter		The Apostle Paul
Emphasis	Mainly Jews	Mixing Jews and Gentiles	Mainly Gentiles
Time	2 years	13 years	15 years
Scope	City Evangelism	Home Missions	Foreign Missions

© 197 Charles R. Swindoll. All rights reserved.
*Main headings adapted from Irving L. Jensen, *Acts: An Independent Study* (Chicago, Ill.: Moody Press, 1968), p. 52.

xiii

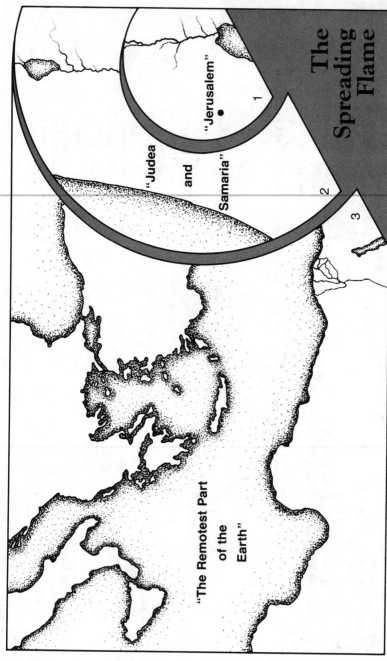

The Spreading Flame

1 "Jerusalem"

2 "Judea and Samaria"

3

"The Remotest Part of the Earth"

"But you shall receive power when the Holy Spirit has come upon you; and you shall be My witnesses both in Jerusalem, and in all Judea and Samaria, and even to the remotest part of the earth." Acts 1:8

Chapter 1

THE SPREADING FLAME

Survey of Acts

A single runner winds his way toward a packed stadium. His is the last leg of a relay that has taken other runners across open farmland, along vast oceans, and through busy city streets. This has been an inspiring journey, one that fulfills an ancient tradition — to carry the Olympic flame.

Now, as this final torchbearer enters a dark passageway and then emerges into the brilliant arena, the crowd erupts in thunderous applause. Holding the flame high, the runner ascends a towering flight of stairs. As he reaches the top, he turns and grandly lights a gigantic torch — the symbol of the Olympic spirit.

The Bible traces a similar relay, only with a different flame — the flame of Christ. The Old Testament patriarchs and prophets carried it bravely, passing it on through each generation until Christ Himself stepped into the world. His flame burned brightly during His ministry on earth, but it exploded in its ultimate glory and power when He conquered death and rose from the grave.

At that time, new torchbearers took Christ's fire into their hearts and began spreading His flame. The book of Acts is their story.

Some Helpful Facts about Acts

As we strike out on our journey to follow these intrepid torchbearers, it is helpful to look ahead and get a feel for where we'll be going. Acts is usually considered one of five historical books in the New Testament. The first four are the Gospels: Matthew, Mark, Luke, and John. These books are all accounts of the life of Christ and are, more accurately, biographies. But Acts is a true history book, putting shoe leather on the gospels so that we can see how the early Christians lived out the teachings of Christ. It is a book

1

filled with fascinating people, life-changing events, and crucial ideas that fly by in a whir of action—hence the title "The *Acts* of the Apostles" (emphasis added).[1]

Referring to his gospel, Luke, the author of Acts, writes, "The first account I composed, Theophilus, about all that Jesus *began* to do and teach" (Acts 1:1, emphasis added). Acts, therefore, is Luke's sequel to his Gospel—what Christ *continued* to do through the Holy Spirit.

Broadly speaking, we can say that Acts is a sequel to the other Gospels as well. Notice how each Gospel ends:

> Matthew: with Christ's *resurrection* (28:1–10)
> Mark: with Christ's *ascension* (16:19)
> Luke: with Christ's *promise of the Holy Spirit* (24:49)
> John: with Christ's *second coming* (21:22)

In the first eleven verses of Acts, the author presents all four of these key themes and shows how they relate to the church. In this way, Acts becomes a bridge, taking us from the life of Christ in the Gospels to the practical theology of the Epistles.

Contrasts between the Gospels and Acts

Acts is a bridge in another sense as well. It spans from the life of Christ to the life of the Christian. In the Gospels, Jesus models Christianity; in Acts, everyday people model Christianity—people like us. In the Gospels, we are Christ's admiring audience; in Acts, we are the ones on stage.

The following chart details more of these contrasts.

Gospels	Acts
We find the Son of God offering His life.	We see Him offering His power.
Original "seeds" of the church are planted: "I will build My church" (Matt. 16:13)	Those seeds take root, begin to sprout, grow, blossom, and bear fruit.

---

1. A better name for the book would be "The Acts of the Holy Spirit," for the author only chronicles the actions of a few of the apostles. Actually the name, "The Acts of the Apostles," was added to the volume in the second century A.D. According to F. F. Bruce, the original title was "History of Christian Origins" and included the Gospel of Luke *and* Acts in one book. *Commentary on the Book of the Acts* (Grand Rapids, Mich.: William B. Eerdmans Publishing Co., 1954), p. 15.

Christ is crucified, risen, and ascended.	Christ is seated in the heavenlies and exalted as head of His body, the church.
We see a personal model of what Christianity is all about (Jesus).	We see human examples of that life fleshed out in ordinary men and women (followers).
The emphasis is on Christ.	The emphasis is on the Holy Spirit.

One man illustrated this when he wrote, "The life that Christ lived qualified Him for the death that He died; and the death that He died qualifies us for the life that He lived." The first part of this statement is the gospel message; the last part is the book of Acts.

The Who and Why of Acts

We can shed more light on Acts by taking a closer look at its author, Luke, and asking him why he wrote this book. We know Luke was a doctor because Paul referred to him as "the beloved physician" (Col. 4:14). Possibly he received his medical training at one of the three universities of his day, which were located in Alexandria, Athens, and Tarsus. The only Gentile writer in the New Testament, Luke was probably Greek, although we do not know his exact place of birth.[2]

He wrote Acts as a sequel to his gospel, addressing the combined work to the same one-man audience—Theophilus (compare Luke 1:1–4 and Acts 1:1).[3] The early church, however, recognized the value of his writings and circulated them widely.

Why did Luke write Acts? Having a passion for history, Dr. Luke endeavored to record a reliable account of the events that followed the ascension of Christ. But his writings are more than just a hodgepodge of minutiae; they comprise a carefully-thought-through history that has a direct bearing on the church today—a bearing that will guide us in understanding the Holy Spirit's ministry in our lives as well.

2. Charles Caldwell Ryrie, *The Acts of the Apostles* (Chicago, Ill.: Moody Press, 1961), p. 8.

3. Theophilus may have been a Greek official in the Roman government who was a new convert to Christianity. Perhaps he was even one of Luke's patients who wanted to understand God's workings in history. See William Barclay, *The Acts of the Apostles*, rev. ed., The Daily Study Bible Series (Philadelphia, Pa.: Westminister Press, 1976), p. 3.

The What and Where of Acts

Chronologically arranged, the contents of the book cover a thirty-year time period—from about A.D. 30, when Jesus ascends to heaven, to A.D. 60, when Paul takes the gospel to Rome. Luke writes some portions of Acts based on his own experiences.[4] The rest of his information comes from other eyewitnesses such as Paul, Silas, and Timothy. "No historian," observes William Barclay, "ever had better sources or used his sources more accurately."[5]

As a result of Luke's meticulousness, Acts is *the* chief sourcebook for information on the coming of the Holy Spirit, the birth of the church, the beginning of world missions, and the spread of Christianity. Like Genesis, Acts is truly a book of beginnings. It records

the first local church,

the first deacons and elders,

the first missions movement,

the first Gentile Christians,

the first use of spiritual gifts,

the first persecutions and martyrs.

Where do the events in Acts take place? Like a travelogue, Acts tours the ancient world—taking us from Jerusalem to what is now Syria and Turkey, then hopscotching across the Mediterranean to Greece and finally Italy.

Geography is key to understanding this book. In fact, it is one of several ways to unlock its outline.

An Easy Outline to Remember

We could outline Acts biographically, focusing on Peter in chapters 1–12 and Paul in chapters 13–28. But the best way to outline the book is geographically, using Acts 1:8 as a guide:

"But you shall receive power when the Holy Spirit has come upon you; and you shall be My witnesses

---

4. Luke was present at many of the events in Acts as evidenced by his use of the pronoun "we." See 16:10–17; 20:5–16; 21:1–18; 27:1–28:16.

5. Barclay, *The Acts of the Apostles*, p. 7.

both in Jerusalem, and in all Judea and Samaria, and even to the remotest part of the earth."

By examining the chart of Acts at the beginning of this guide, you can see how this verse truly summarizes the entire book. Chapters 1–7 describe *the church established at Jerusalem.* In this phase, which lasted about two years, the Jewish Christians were Christ's witnesses mainly to other Jews. They were involved in what we might call "city evangelism."

Then, after this phase, a tornado of trouble hit.

> And on that day a great persecution arose against the church in Jerusalem; and they were all scattered throughout the regions of Judea and Samaria, except the apostles. (8:1b)

The Holy Spirit used this persecution to push the believers beyond their secure walls and into the surrounding countryside. As a result, *the church scattered to Judea and Samaria* (chaps. 8–12).

For thirteen years, these believers took the gospel to their Gentile neighbors. This was an uncomfortable, stretching time of transition for the Christian Jews. We would say that they were involved in "home missions." The world still lay at the doorstep, so the Holy Spirit moved once more.

> Now there were at Antioch, in the church that was there, prophets and teachers: Barnabas, and Simeon who was called Niger, and Lucius of Cyrene, and Manaen who had been brought up with Herod the tetrarch, and Saul. And while they were ministering to the Lord and fasting, the Holy Spirit said, "Set apart for Me Barnabas and Saul for the work to which I have called them." Then, when they had fasted and prayed and laid their hands on them, they sent them away. (13:1–3)

The first missionaries were commissioned to carry the flame of Christ to foreign counties. As a result, *the church extended to the remotest part of the earth.* This was the advent of "foreign missions," with the apostle Paul evangelizing the Gentiles in city after city. This period ended about fifteen years later, as Paul awaited an audience with Caesar in Rome,

> preaching the kingdom of God, and teaching con-

cerning the Lord Jesus Christ with all openness, unhindered. (28:31)

An Essential Book to Apply

So far, we've seen Acts from a bird's-eye view. From that perspective, Luke's story of the church remarkably resembles our own
Christian development. For we, too, go through stages of establishing, scattering, and extending.

Establishing. As new Christians, we enter a period of putting
down roots. It's a nurturing time when Christ holds us close to
Himself, often protecting us from many of life's pains and giving us
a sturdy foundation. Then, according to His timetable, the next
phase begins.

Scattering. Persecution and pain, discomfort and disappointment
are the watermarks of this stage, as Christ allows trials to wash over
our lives. This time may bring a literal scattering—moving away
from family and friends—as a result of layoffs at work or changes
in careers. Or it may mean an emotional scattering—a deep suffering that comes from broken relationships or topsy-turvy circumstances. Through such times, the Lord strengthens us so that,
eventually, we enter another phase of life.

Extending. Having profited from life's buffeting, we become sea-
soned, mature servants of Christ—cracks and all. Here He uses us
as proven and worthy vessels that overflow with the message of
Christ's power, unhindered.

The book of Acts ends with Paul under house arrest, yet still
proclaiming Christ with his every breath. His ministry was not over,
and neither was Acts. "The Book of Acts," it has been said, "is an
unfinished book, for it is still being written"[6]—in your life and the
lives of all Christians who carry Christ's flame into a darkened world.

☀ *Living Insights* STUDY ONE

STUDY ONE

Being Christ's torchbearer begins in your Jerusalem—your
hometown. This is your most immediate circle of influence, the
place where your family and friends see your Christianity in action.

6. Ray Stedman, *Birth of the Body* (Santa Ana, Calif.: Vision House Publishers, 1974), p. 15.

In what ways can you reveal the flame of Christ to them?

_____

_____

Your second circle of influence is your Judea and Samaria. For you, "Samaritans" may be people from a different ethnic group, the homeless, or even those in prison. How can you or your church show them Christ's love?

_____

_____

Third, broadening the circle to encompass the world, you can reveal Christ to those in the remotest parts of the earth. In what ways can you become involved in world missions through your local church?

_____

_____

In each of these circles of influence, you can be a torchbearer— one who carries the flame of Christ to those who need its warmth and hope.

☀ Living Insights STUDY TWO

Like the early church, we go through phases. Which one do you think you're in now?

❏ Establishing   ❏ Scattering   ❏ Extending

What characteristics of this phase describe your life?

_____

_____

Whether God is establishing, scattering, or extending you, you can be sure of one thing, "that He who began a good work in you will perfect it until the day of Christ Jesus" (Phil. 1:6b). God will bring to maturity the work He started in your life. How do you think He can use this phase you're going through now to produce further growth in your life?

_____

_____

_____

Through this process, you must be willing to trust His plan for you. This takes faith—the kind aptly illustrated by Charles Haddon Spurgeon:

> Let us lean on God with all our weight. Let us throw ourselves on his faithfulness as we do on our beds, bringing all our weariness to his dear rest.[7]

Lean on God by expressing your trust in Him to bring you through this and subsequent stages of life (read Ps. 37:5–6, and Prov. 3:5–6).

———◆———

Dear Father,

_____

_____

_____

_____

_____

_____

_____

_____

_____

7. Charles Haddon Spurgeon, *Spurgeon at His Best*, comp. Tom Carter (Grand Rapids, Mich.: Baker Book House, 1988), p. 210.

Chapter 2

OPERATION REVOLUTION
Acts 1:1–14

In the last few decades, a technological revolution has swept through and, like a cloudburst, has rained on us torrents of change. In the years to come, technology will further deluge us, affecting the way we think, the way we relate, the way we live.

Soon many recent innovations will be commonplace. At the touch of a button, we'll have unlimited access to libraries of information. Shopping malls will be condensed to a home video disk for our televisions. Our cars will be rolling offices equipped with fax machines, mini-microwaves, and video maps to guide us around traffic jams.

"Smart" houses will know who is in each room, adjusting the temperature accordingly. Family rooms will resemble control booths, with high-definition television and entree to a global entertainment market. Video games will be three-dimensional, utilizing a concept called "virtual reality." Players will actually have the ability to step *inside* the game, entering the ultimate adventure fantasy.

Scientists are even forecasting a society based on artificial intelligence, robotics, and genetic engineering. What will it be like to program a computer to think the way you do, or swallow a micro-robot that doctors can guide to perform surgery, or wipe out genetic diseases like cystic fibrosis and Down's syndrome? These are all possibilities as we career toward the year 2000 and beyond.[1]

Our world is changing, but as Christians we should not be threatened. For we are part of another revolution, one that began two thousand years ago: the church. No political or technological revolution can alter its course or defeat its purpose. Even "the gates of hell shall not overpower it" (Matt. 16:18b).

Why is the church so powerful? How can ordinary Christians revolutionize a high-tech world? Is it really possible for us to be

This lesson has drawn much material from Ray Stedman's *Acts 1–12: Birth of the Body* (Santa Ana, Calif.: Vision House Publishers, 1974), pp. 11–24.

1. See Russell Chandler, *Racing toward 2001* (published by Grand Rapids, Mich.: Zondervan Publishing House and San Francisco, Calif.: HarperSanFrancisco, 1992), pp. 48, 50–53, 57–58, 65.

pacesetters for our generation and the generations to come? To find the answers to these questions, we must look to Christ, the founder of the church, and to a concept called the Incarnation.

Importance of the Incarnation

Beginning where the book of Acts starts, we immediately come across the central figure of Luke's writings, the Son of God.

Christ Jesus

Referring to the Gospel bearing his name, Luke writes,

> The first account I composed, Theophilus, about all that Jesus began to do and teach. (Acts 1:1)

The Gospel of Luke portrays Jesus as the incarnate Son of God — the living, eternal, all-powerful God of heaven dressed in human garb. Here in flesh and blood was God in all His power, rubbing shoulders with humanity. But Luke and the other Gospel accounts narrate only the beginning of Jesus' ministry on earth; Acts describes its continuation through His Spirit-empowered followers.

> In the Gospels He did it in His own physical body, but in the Book of Acts he is doing it through the bodies of men and women who are indwelt by His life. Whether in the Gospels or in Acts, *incarnation is the secret strategy by which God changes the world.*[2] (emphasis added)

Christ in us, working through us by the power of the Holy Spirit—that's incarnation. And among the first to experience it were the apostles.

Chosen Apostles

Jesus, on "the day when He was taken up" (v. 2a), ascended into heaven; but before He left the earth,

> He had by the Holy Spirit given orders to the apostles whom He had chosen. (v. 2b)

2. Ray Stedman, *Acts 1–12: Birth of the Body* (Santa Ana, Calif.: Vision House Publishers, 1974), p. 14.

Although the Incarnate One would soon leave, His message would go on—not through an angel or through God's booming voice, but through frail, fallible humans. Christ's humble, ordinary followers would carry out a revolution that only the God of the universe could engineer.

Plan for Revolution

Christ developed His strategy for revolution from two key events in His life on earth. These events form the historical basis of His plan.

Historical Basis

One of these events was *His resurrection*. Demonstrating the unconquerable power of God, Christ's resurrection was and is the most significant fact of Christianity. But did it really happen? The third verse leaves little doubt.

> To [the apostles] He also presented Himself alive, after His suffering, by many convincing proofs, appearing to them over a period of forty days, and speaking of the things concerning the kingdom of God.

From this verse, "many convincing proofs" confirm the Resurrection.

Not only did those early Christians see Jesus in His resurrected body, but they were with Him over a period of time—they didn't just have some kind of momentary hallucination. And they not only saw Him, they heard Him speak. The evidence is irrefutable. Jesus died and He rose again; visibly and audibly He proved it.

Overcoming death—what power! And the power that enabled Christ to walk out of His own grave is present today inside each believer. How is this possible?

The answer is found in the other event—one that took place before His resurrection and even before His death—His farewell discourse in the Upper Room, in which He gave *the promise of the Father*:

> "Truly, truly, I say to you, he who believes in Me, the works that I do shall he do also; and greater works than these shall he do; because I go to the Father. And whatever you ask in My name, that will

I do, that the Father may be glorified in the Son. If you ask Me anything in My name, I will do it. If you love Me, you will keep My commandments. And I will ask the Father, and He will give you another Helper, that He may be with you forever; that is the Spirit of truth, whom the world cannot receive, because it does not behold Him or know Him, but you know Him because He abides with you, and will be in you." (John 14:12–17)

The power that filled Christ in His earthly ministry would soon fill the disciples and, later, us (see 1 Cor. 12:13). At the Resurrection, there was a *release* of power; afterwards there was the *transfer* of power Christ spoke of in the Upper Room. Gathering the apostles together before His transfiguration, Jesus instructed them to simply wait for this transfer to occur (Acts 1:4).

Revolution often comes in the form of military machines or manipulative propaganda. But not Christ's. His revolution was empowered by four dynamics that just might surprise you.

Dynamic Elements

The dynamic elements of the revolutionary church are not as much external flash as internal vitality, as we see in verses 5–8. The first is that the church is *not a symbol but a reality*. Quoting Jesus, Luke writes,

> "For John baptized with water, but you shall be baptized with the Holy Spirit not many days from now."
> (v. 5)

John baptized people as a symbol of their desire to identify themselves with the Messiah's ministry and purpose.[3] As the Messiah, though, Jesus promised an altogether different baptism—a baptism not with water but with a Person, the Holy Spirit.

As a result of this baptism, the One who empowered Christ now indwells us at the point of salvation (see Rom. 8:9). This spiritual baptism is something that cannot be earned. It is God's gift of Himself to us, so that, as Ray Stedman puts it, "all that Jesus is, is

---

3. The Greek word for baptism is *baptizō*, which "metaphorically meant to change identity, to change appearance, or even to change relationships." J. Dwight Pentecost, *The Words and Works of Jesus Christ* (Grand Rapids, Mich.: Zondervan Publishing House, 1981), p. 83.

made available through all that I am."[4]

Second, Jesus' words to the disciples teach us that the church is *not a program but a power.*

> And so when they had come together, they were asking Him, saying, "Lord, is it at this time You are restoring the kingdom to Israel?" He said to them, "It is not for you to know times or epochs which the Father has fixed by His own authority; but you shall receive power when the Holy Spirit has come upon you." (Acts 1:6–8a)

Preoccupied with the tangible facets of the kingdom, the disciples wanted program information—the where, when, and how of God's revolution. But God doesn't incarnate Himself in a program; rather, He houses Himself in human beings, encasing His power in flesh for everyone to see and touch.

What is the nature of this power? Is it blaring, pounding, frightening? On the contrary, God's power is quiet. Like a policeman at an intersection, who merely raises his hand to stop fast-moving traffic, God says the word, and by His authority His will is done.

He requires no clever programs. He has no bag of tricks, no eye-catching gimmicks to influence others. On the contrary,

> resurrection power changes lives from *within* rather than from without. . . . It does not separate or divide; it harmonizes, heals, draws people together, and breaks down walls of hostility that have been standing sometimes for centuries. It batters these all down and brings people together in harmony. This totally different kind of power is what you receive when you receive the Holy Spirit.[5]

Third, Jesus' church members are *not promoters but witnesses.* He says specifically,

> "And you shall be My witnesses both in Jerusalem, and in all Judea and Samaria, and even to the remotest part of the earth." (v. 8b)

4. Stedman, *Acts 1–12*, p. 20. See Acts 2:38; Eph. 3:14–19.
5. Stedman, *Acts 1–12*, p. 21.

Witnesses are people who simply tell what they have experienced. Similarly, as witnesses for Christ, we just tell others that we know Christ saves because He has saved us. "Christians are not to be like salesmen going out to peddle a product," writes Ray Stedman,

> nor are they to be recruiters trying to get people to join a religious club. By doing this the church has become false and has lost its power. . . .
>
> The mark of a carnal church is that it loves to talk about itself. These early Christians never witnessed about the church at all; they witnessed about the Lord—what He could do, how He would work, what a fantastic person He was, how amazing His power was, and what He could do in human hearts.[6]

Fourth, the church is *not restricted but universal*. From Jerusalem to the "remotest part of the earth" (v. 8b), the church spreads. It fits into any culture, alongside any race or class of people. And it is timeless, relevant then, now, and in the future as well.

Authentic Assurance

The future has always been an essential aspect of God's revolutionary plan. Christ demonstrated God's power at His resurrection; we incarnate His power today . . . but in the future, Christ will return to Earth to reveal, once and for all, His supremacy. This hope was issued to the disciples present at Christ's ascension.

> He was lifted up while they were looking on, and a cloud received Him out of their sight. And as they were gazing intently into the sky while He was departing, behold, two men in white clothing stood beside them; and they also said, "Men of Galilee, why do you stand looking into the sky? This Jesus, who has been taken up from you into heaven, will come in just the same way as you have watched Him go into heaven." (vv. 9b–11)

The assurance that Christ will return someday sparks in us a desire to obey Him, a desire felt by the disciples as well.

---

6. Stedman, *Acts 1–12*, p. 21.

Specific Obedience

They returned immediately to Jerusalem and "went up to the upper room, where they were staying" and "were continually devoting themselves to prayer" (vv. 12–14). Rather than attempting to spread the gospel without the Holy Spirit's power, they waited for the moment when God's incarnation strategy would begin—when the Holy Spirit would fill them with the spiritual vitality needed to go out and change their world.

Principles of Appropriation

In many ways, our world is vastly different than that of the early Christians, but in other respects nothing has changed. Technologically, we've never been so advanced; but people still die of hunger, felons still commit brutal crimes, and millions still are emotionally and spiritually empty.

In light of this fact, two implications of Christ's revolutionary incarnation strategy remain true:

- *To implement an effective plan, people must be infected.* It is not enough to talk about the gospel; people must experience it through us. One on one. Person to person. Christ incarnated in us can change people's lives.

- *To impact an advanced world, power must be released.* The disciples were a group of relatively ignorant men who shaped their world because the power of God was released in their lives. In the uncertain days ahead, may our society thus change as a result of the mighty but quiet wave of God's Spirit in us.

☀ Living Insights   STUDY ONE

The book of Acts is a study in revolution. We often think of a revolution in political or military terms—slogans scrawled across buildings, iron-jawed leaders shouting defiance, boys in fatigues carrying terrible weapons. Christ's revolution in Acts, though, contrasts with these images. He builds love, not hate; peace, not turmoil; forgiveness, not spite; gentleness, not anger; life, not death.

How would you describe your heart lately? Has it been a battleground of strife or a scene of peace? Explain why.

15

_____

_____

_____

Just as a military overthrow can inject fear and compliance into the hearts of a nation, so also a spiritual coup can infuse patience, self-control, and hope. Meditate on 2 Cor. 5:17; Col. 3:12–17, and write down some ways in which the life-giving characteristics of Christ in you can revolutionize your life.

_____

_____

_____

_____

☀ *Living Insights*   STUDY TWO

Christ's spiritual revolution brings about change from the inside out. His change begins with the soul, altering in turn the individual, the family, the community, and finally shifting the course of society. Benjamin Franklin admitted: "He who introduces into public affairs the principles of primitive Christianity will change the face of the world."[7]

Through this study in Acts, you will see how the early Christians changed their world. "But things are different now," some may object. "How can Christianity change my home or my town or my country?"

Well, daydream about this for a minute. What would your family be like if all your relatives were Christians? Write down some differences you'd see.

_____

_____

_____

7. Benjamin Franklin, as quoted by Bill Bright in *Revolution Now* (San Bernardino, Calif.: Campus Crusade for Christ, 1969), p. 22.

What would your public school system be like if more Christians sat on the Board of Education? If more of the principals and teachers were Christians?

_____

_____

What would your city be like if the mayor and city council members were Christians?

_____

_____

What would this country be like if government officials were followers of Christ?

_____

_____

Is such a vision merely a utopian ideal? It is—if we do nothing about it. It isn't, though, if we are willing to follow Christ's imperative:

> "But you shall receive power when the Holy Spirit has come upon you; and you shall be My witnesses both in Jerusalem, and in all Judea and Samaria, and even to the remotest part of the earth." (Acts 1:8)

How can you begin to enact this vision of change today?

_____

_____

_____

Chapter 3

DICE IN THE PRAYER MEETING

Acts 1:12–26

Before becoming a screen star, young Burt Lancaster was a circus performer—a job he was fortunate to land, considering his less-than-flawless audition.

> He was asked to perform on the parallel bars, so he leaped on the bars and began his routine. Because he was nervous, his timing was off, and he spun over the bar, falling flat on his face some 10 feet below. He was so humiliated that he immediately leaped back on the bar. As he spun again at the same point, he flipped off and smashed to the ground once more!
>
> Burt's tights were torn, he was cut and bleeding, and he was fiercely upset! He leaped back again, but the third time was even worse, for this time he fell on his back. The agent came over, picked him up, and said, "Son, if you won't do that again, you've got the job!"[1]

Doesn't this image of Burt Lancaster spinning, crashing, and coming back for more mirror our own Christian life at times? With determined self-sufficiency, we leap into this venture and that, teeter, and then flop face-first onto the ground. Then what do we do? We brush off the sawdust and go at it again, falling even harder the next time.

Finally, God comes over and says, "My child, if you won't do that again, you've got the job—I can use you!"

After Christ's ascension, the disciples may have been tempted to mount the bars and start performing on their own strength. But they didn't. Trusting God to give them His power according to His plan and His timing, they waited. This is what we find them doing in today's lesson.

1. Robert L. Wise, *Your Churning Place* (Glendale, Calif.: G/L Publications, Regal Books, 1977), p. 66.

Who Was Where, and Why?

These first followers of Jesus were saintly men and women of iron will and relentless faith . . . right? On the contrary; they were ordinary and imperfect. Let's peek into the room where they were gathered and see who they were.

The People

Gathered together was a group of 120 people. Of that group (Acts 1:15), we know a few by name, as well as by their track records. Peter, who had denied Christ, was there. John and his brother James, who had wanted special seats in the kingdom, were there too. Andrew, Philip, and Thomas (the Doubter) were present, as well as Matthew (the tax collector), Simon (the Zealot), Bartholomew, James (the son of Alphaeus), and Judas, the son of James (v. 13). Also among them were Jesus' brothers (v. 14b), who earlier had scoffed at Him and even thought that He was insane (see John 7:3–5 and Mark 3:21).

All in all, it was a bunch of failing, often faithless people. No halos hovered over anyone in this list. Yet these were the ones God planned to empower with His Holy Spirit. God never requires perfection or impressive resumes from those He wants to use. In fact, He often chooses unlikely, face-in-the-dust people . . . people just like us.

The Place

Where was this unlikely group gathered? Acts 1:13 tells us that after the Ascension, "they went up to the Upper Room, where they were staying." Probably a familiar meeting place for them, the Upper Room was the second floor of a large house in Jerusalem.[2]

The Purpose

Here, they were following Jesus' instructions, waiting for the baptism of the Holy Spirit that Jesus had promised (vv. 4–5). They

---

2. The article "the" indicates that this room was a specific place, one in which they may have often met. "Whether this particular room should be identified with that where the Last Supper was held (Luke 22:12—a different Greek word for 'room' is used) and located in the house of Mary, the mother of John Mark (12:12), cannot be stated with any certainty." See I. Howard Marshall, The Acts of the Apostles, The Tyndale New Testament Commentaries series (1980; reprint, Leicester, England: Inter-Varsity Press, 1983; Grand Rapids, Mich.: William B. Eerdmans Publishing Co., 1983), p. 62.

knew that without this spiritual power they could never fulfill His command to be witnesses to the world (v. 8). So they stayed together and waited, but they weren't idle.

> These all with one mind were continually devoting themselves to prayer. (v. 14a)

Notice first that they were of "one mind." Commenting on the unity these Christians experienced, Lloyd John Ogilvie writes:

> I have always felt that Pentecost happened not according to a date on a calendar but in response to reconciliation among the disciples. There were deep tensions among them during and after Jesus' ministry. . . . Until they were together on their knees, fully open to God and each other, the Holy Spirit could not be given.[3]

Second, they were "devoting themselves to prayer." What were they praying for? We don't know exactly, but possibly their fervent prayer went something like this: "Lord, send your Spirit, baptize us in your power, fulfill Your promise soon, and let us know what it means to have the Holy Spirit within us."

Is this a prayer that should be on our lips today? Should we seek to be baptized by the Holy Spirit for power as some teachers suggest? No, we should not. These early believers were in a brief, unrepeatable period between the promise of the Spirit and the giving of the Spirit. At His ascension, Jesus told them that power was coming (v. 8), and about a week later it came. Ever since then, believers have been immediately baptized in the Spirit at the moment of salvation (1 Cor. 12:13).

An illustration may help clarify this important issue. Suppose you choose to start a corporation, and you need ten people to serve on the board of directors. You promise to give each of them five thousand dollars if they agree to sit on the board, but it will take some time to put together all the arrangements. So each person waits anxiously for the opening of the corporation and the promised check. Once you launch the company and need additional board members, though, the new people don't have to wait for their checks. They receive them immediately, because the company has already begun.

3. Lloyd John Ogilvie, *Drumbeat of Love* (Waco, Tex.: Word Books, 1976), p. 20.

Like the original board members, these first Christians had to wait for the church to begin and the Spirit to be poured out in order to receive God's power. But today, since the church is in place and the Holy Spirit has been given, we already have the Spirit—we have our check in hand. Christians may plead to God to write them the check. But God says, "You have it, just *cash it!*"

What Was When, and How?

Because these early believers didn't yet have the Spirit, they continued to pray and wait. In the middle of their prayers, however, Peter realized something was missing.

The Need

So he stood up and said:

> "Brethren, the Scripture had to be fulfilled, which the Holy Spirit foretold by the mouth of David concerning Judas, who became a guide to those who arrested Jesus. For he was counted among us, and received his portion in this ministry." (Now this man acquired a field with the price of his wickedness; and falling headlong, he burst open in the middle and all his bowels gushed out. And it became known to all who were living in Jerusalem; so that in their own language that field was called Hakeldama, that is, Field of Blood.) "For it is written in the book of Psalms,
> 'Let his homestead be made desolate,
> And let no man dwell in it';
> and,
> 'His office let another man take.'
> It is therefore necessary that of the men who have accompanied us all the time that the Lord Jesus went in and out among us—beginning with the baptism of John, until the day that He was taken up from us—one of these should become a witness with us of His resurrection." (Acts 1:16–22)

When Judas Iscariot betrayed Jesus and then committed suicide, he forfeited his position as one of the twelve apostles. Someone must take his place so there could be twelve apostles again. But why was this so important?

Earlier, Jesus had made a significant promise to the disciples:

> "Truly I say to you, that you who have followed Me,
> in the regeneration when the Son of Man will sit
> on His glorious throne, you also shall sit upon twelve
> thrones, judging the twelve tribes of Israel."
> (Matt. 19:28)

The twelfth apostle was required to be one of the future judges of Israel. But who? Jesus had selected the original men, but He wasn't there. This new apostle (1) had to "have accompanied us all the time that the Lord Jesus went in and out among us" (Acts 1:21); and (2) had to have seen the resurrected Christ (v. 22b).

The Time

So they dealt with the problem immediately. Right then, they began choosing the twelfth apostle by judging the candidates according to these two qualifications.

The Method

As a result,

> they put forward two men, Joseph called Barsabbas
> (who was also called Justus), and Matthias. (v. 23)

Two men met the prerequisites, Joseph Barsabbas, who was also called Justus, and Matthias. How would they choose between them?

> They prayed, and said, "Thou, Lord, who knowest
> the hearts of all men, show which one of these two
> Thou hast chosen to occupy this ministry and apos-
> tleship from which Judas turned aside to go to his
> own place." And they drew lots for them, and the
> lot fell to Matthias; and he was numbered with the
> eleven apostles. (vv. 24–26)

Not yet having the personal guidance of the Holy Spirit, they prayed and then utilized an Old Testament method of determining God's will—drawing lots. Charles Ryrie explains how this was done.

> They prayed not for the Lord to choose but for the
> choice which the Lord had already made to be made
> known to them. The two names were put on lots,

22

placed in an urn, and then the one which first fell
from the urn was taken to be the Lord's choice.[4]

According to Proverbs 16:33, "The lot is cast into the lap, But
its every decision is from the Lord." So, for them, drawing lots was
a reliable way to determine God's choice. But what about us today?
To find out God's will should we draw straws or flip coins or throw
darts?

No, we don't need to employ such decision-making methods
because we have the Holy Spirit's voice within us and the Holy
Scripture to guide us. In fact, this was the last time God directed
His people through this method. And as a result, the twelfth apostle
was chosen, Matthias.

Who Cares? So What?

Jesus' followers were on the verge of an earthshaking event that
would change the way God related to men and women everywhere.
Soon, at Pentecost, the Holy Spirit would burst into the hearts of
believers for the first time, forever altering their lives and ours.

These Upper Room events formed an indispensable prelude to
that forthcoming power—a prelude that featured two integral principles for Christian living.

First, *the people God empowers are not perfect performers but dependent believers.* The original 120 men and women were not perfect;
they had faulty and frayed pasts. Yet . . . they believed God. Today
many of us live under a heavy standard called perfectionism. But
God is not looking for flashy, flawless circus performers; rather, He
uses those who climb off the performance bars and simply trust Him.

Second, *the plan God honors is not complicated but simple.* God
said, "Go to Jerusalem and wait." And they went to Jerusalem and
waited. He said, "Trust Me to send the power." And they trusted
Him. Then He said, "Call on Me and I'll tell you who My choice
is for the twelfth apostle." And they did. No one in the Upper
Room disputed God's choice of Matthias. Their obedience to God's
simple path is a model of how we should walk with Jesus as well.

4. Charles Caldwell Ryrie, *The Acts of the Apostles* (Chicago, Ill.: Moody Press, 1961), p. 16.

In the Olympics, perfection is measured not in seconds or points but in hundredths of seconds and hundredths of points. How fast is one hundredth of a second? How close is one hundredth of a point? So fast and so close that, normally, it matters little. Except when perfection is measured.

Some of us measure our lives by hundredths. One wrong word said and we deduct a hundredth. One mistake at work or at home . . . two more hundredths. One slipup, one inadequacy, one miscalculation . . . the hundredths tick away, becoming sad, red-penciled minuses displayed for all to see.

Do you measure your life by such perfectionistic standards? In what areas especially?

_____

_____

Fortunately, however, *the people God empowers are not the perfect performers but those who depend on Him.* Meditate on this passage:

> "God is opposed to the proud, but gives grace to the humble." Submit therefore to God. Resist the devil and he will flee from you. Draw near to God and He will draw near to you. (James 4:6b–8a)

Draw near to Him today. Depend on Him. And . . . give away your stopwatch!

☀ *Living Insights*   STUDY TWO

Who said Sunday is a day of rest? Most Sundays, our alarm clocks ring early and we're off to the races. Lap 1 is just getting out of the house slicked down, spritzed up, and squeaky clean. Screeching into the parking lot, lap 2 begins as we race in and out of church flashing a few Hollywood smiles. Lap 3—back to the house for pot roast and off to church again for choir practice and committee meeting. *Home stretch!* Prayer time. Evening worship. Fellowship hour. Say good-bye. Kids to bed. Dishes. Vacuum. Whew—the finish line. Bed.

We've been programmed to think that fatigue is next to godliness. That the more exhausted we are (and look!), the more spiritual we are and the more we earn God's smile of approval. We bury all thoughts of enjoying life . . . for we all know that committed, truly committed, Christians are those who work, work, work. Preferably, with great intensity. As a result, we have become a generation of people who worship our work, who work at our play, and who play at our worship.[5]

God's plan for us, however, is not as complicated and exhausting as we make it. It's simple. Sometimes it's even just waiting. But how do we determine how busy our Christian life should be?

First, list all your involvements. If these lines are not enough, you know already that you're too busy!

_____

_____

Now, list what you know God wants you to be doing. For examples, look up John 13:35; Acts 1:8,14; and 2 Timothy 2:15.

_____

_____

Finally, compare God's list with your list. Maybe there are some areas in which you could cut back to follow God's plan more closely. Or perhaps, for a time, you could focus on just one of God's commands—prayer, for instance. Write down your ideas.

_____

_____

_____

Is your life too complicated, too busy? Someone did say we should have a day of rest. Don't forget to take Him up on it.

---

5. Charles R. Swindoll, *Leisure* (Portland, Oreg.: Multnomah Press, 1981), pp. 4–5.

Chapter 4

SUPERNATURAL CHURCHBIRTH

Acts 2:1–13

Stories of the supernatural bring out the skeptic in all of us. If it can't be scrutinized, analyzed, or categorized, we don't believe it. Maybe we've seen too many tabloids touting Miss So-and-so's recent date with Elvis. Or perhaps we've heard too many stories like the one that came out of Russell, Kansas. A woman there says she spoke with several extraterrestrials, including one who drove a Rolls-Royce with California tags![1]

Claims such as these make it difficult to believe that supernatural events actually occur. This lesson focuses on one such event. It's not a UFO sighting, but the situation is similar. God the Holy Spirit invaded the hearts of men and women in an amazing, unrepeatable way.

"But if we can't explain it," our skepticism protests, "how do we know it really happened?"

The account in Acts 2 of what occurred at Pentecost gives us convincing evidence that something unearthly did happen then. But this passage gives us much more—it confirms our own supernatural relationship with God, who gives His Spirit to all who believe in Jesus Christ.

Some Background Information

God's gift of the Holy Spirit was the fulfillment of several promises Jesus made prior to the Day of Pentecost.

The Promises of Jesus

On the eve of His crucifixion, Jesus reassured the disciples that "another Helper" would come.

> "And I will ask the Father, and He will give you another Helper, that He may be with you forever; that is the Spirit of truth, whom the world cannot

---

1. Kevin Helliker, "Odd Tales of UFOs and Sen. Bob Dole Visit Russell, Kan.," *The Wall Street Journal*, October 15, 1991, p. 1.

receive, because it does not behold Him or know Him, but you know Him because He abides with you, and will be in you." (John 14:16–17)

At that time, they had only seen the power of the Holy Spirit externally. But soon they would experience it internally—as Jesus told them, He "will be in you."

During the forty days after Jesus' death and resurrection, He appeared to the disciples several times. At the end of that period, just before His ascension, Jesus restated His promise, giving a few more details.

"For John baptized with water, but you shall be baptized with the Holy Spirit not many days from now. . . . You shall receive power when the Holy Spirit has come upon you; and you shall be My witnesses." (Acts 1:5, 8a)

The disciples would be baptized with the Spirit, would receive His internal power, would be Christ's witnesses to the world. Jesus told them what would happen, but He didn't tell them how, nor did He tell them exactly when. It caught them by surprise on a very significant day of the Jewish calendar.

The Day of Pentecost

The second chapter of Acts opens with, "When the day of Pentecost had come" (Acts 2:1a). Why is this day important? Bible scholar F. F. Bruce gives us some interesting background information:

The day of Pentecost was so called because it was celebrated on the fiftieth (Gk. *pentekostos*) day after the presentation of the first harvested sheaf of the barley harvest, *i.e.* the fiftieth day from the first Sunday after Passover (*cf.* Lev. 23:15f.). It was known among Hebrew-speaking people as the "feast of weeks" . . . and also as "the day of the first-fruits" . . . because it was the day when "the first-fruits of wheat harvest" (Ex. 34:22a) were presented to God.[2]

2. F. F. Bruce, ed., *Commentary on the Book of the Acts*, The New International Commentary on the New Testament series (Grand Rapids, Mich.: William B. Eerdmans Publishing Co., 1954), pp. 53–54.

Jews from every nation had come to Jerusalem to celebrate the harvest of the firstfruits. God chose that day to bring forth the church and initiate a worldwide spiritual harvest. This was all done in the name of Jesus, who was "raised from the dead, the first fruits of those who are asleep" (1 Cor. 15:20).

The Unity of Believers

For this harvest to begin, Jesus' followers needed a unity of spirit. According to Luke, these believers were of "one mind" (Acts 1:14) and "were all together in one place" (2:1b). Or, as the King James Version reads, "they were all with one accord in one place." Earlier, Jesus had prayed for His followers to enjoy such harmony:

> "I do not ask in behalf of these alone, but for those also who believe in Me through their word; that they may all be one; even as Thou, Father, art in Me, and I in Thee, that they also may be in Us; that the world may believe that Thou didst send Me." (John 17:20–21)

Now His prayer was being answered. Believers were coming together, not in uniformity but in unity. They had varied backgrounds, training, and temperaments, yet despite their differences they had become one.

Evidences of the Spirit's Coming

All the preparations had been made: Jesus had given His promise, the perfect day was at hand, and God's people were enjoying an unparalleled sweetness of fellowship. Then . . . it happened.

Audible Evidence

A noise came "suddenly," as Luke describes it (Acts 2:2). Unlike the arrival of a tornado or hurricane, which often can be forecasted, this noise came like an earthquake, without warning. And, Luke writes, it "came from heaven" (v. 2a). This was no earthly, man-made sound. Instead, it was

> a noise like a violent, rushing wind, and it filled the whole house where they were sitting. (v. 2b)

Our word *echo* comes from the Greek word for *noise* used in this verse. As A. T. Robertson explains, it was "an echoing sound as of a mighty wind borne violently."[3] It wasn't the wind, but it *sounded* like the rushing of the wind. Like the deep, deafening roar of a Boeing 747 at take-off, the noise must have shaken the house down to its foundation. But that wasn't all—they saw something too.

Visible Evidence

> There appeared to them tongues as of fire distribut-
> ing themselves, and they rested on each one of them.
> (v. 3)

To their amazement, firelike manifestations resembling tongues settled on each person. Soon their own tongues would seem to be on fire as the Holy Spirit empowered them to proclaim the gospel in a supernatural way.

Oral Evidence

Unmistakably, the Holy Spirit was in the noise and the fire—both external manifestations. But when the flame rested on each person,

> they were all *filled* with the Holy Spirit and began
> to speak with other tongues, as the Spirit was giving
> them utterance. (v. 4, emphasis added)

Imagine their surprise when they began conversing in other languages![4] This was audible evidence that the Holy Spirit indwelt each of them personally.

Not only could they speak in languages previously unknown to them, but they also used the proper dialects (see v. 8b). In this way, the newborn church made its first infant cry, joyously proclaiming the gospel of Christ in words the whole world could understand.

Reactions to the Spirit's Coming

The Spirit's rumblings in that Upper Room spilled out into the

3. Archibald Thomas Robertson, *Word Pictures in the New Testament* (Grand Rapids, Mich.: Baker Book House, 1930), vol. 3, p. 20.

4. They spoke "with other tongues" (v. 4). The Greek word for *other* is *heteros* which denotes a "qualitative difference" and "involves the . . . idea of difference in kind." G. Abbott-Smith, *A Manual Greek Lexicon of the New Testament*, 3d ed. (Edinburgh, Scotland: T. and T. Clark, 1937), p. 22. Therefore they spoke in a different tongue or language than they had previously known.

street below. Thousands crowded around, coming to find out what had made such a tremendous noise. Then, the 120 followers of Christ emerged, speaking more languages than you'd hear at the Olympics. Luke describes the people's responses to this phenomenon.

Confusion

> Now there were Jews living in Jerusalem, devout men, from every nation under heaven. And when this sound occurred, the multitude came together, and were bewildered, because they were each one hearing them speak in his own language. (vv. 5–6)

The Pentecost celebration had drawn Jews from every country and culture. Never before had they heard their languages spoken so well outside their own countries, and their first response was bewilderment. Is there any wonder?

Amazement

Their confusion turned into amazement when they realized that those speaking their languages were Galileans.

> And they were amazed and marveled, saying, "Why, are not all these who are speaking Galileans?" (v. 7)

Literally, they "kept on being amazed." As they listened, their mouths dropped open and they shook their heads. This was incredible! Uneducated, backwoods Galileans, who usually roughed up their own language, could speak the languages of the world better than their own mother tongue.

Curiosity

Curiosity overtook their amazement as they began searching for the meaning behind this miracle.

> "How is it that we each hear them in our own language to which we were born? Parthians and Medes and Elamites, and residents of Mesopotamia, Judea and Cappadocia, Pontus and Asia, Phrygia, and Pamphylia, Egypt and the districts of Libya around Cyrene, and visitors from Rome, both Jews and proselytes, Cretans and Arabs—we hear them in our own tongues speaking of the mighty deeds of God."

And they continued in amazement and great per-
plexity, saying to one another, "What does this
mean?" (vv. 8–12)

The people knew that the Galileans had been supernaturally
changed, not only because they heard them fluently speak foreign
languages, but also because they spoke with such confidence. They
used to be frightened mice, hiding and huddling together. Now they
were lions, roaring out the "mighty deeds of God."

Today, some people say we need another Pentecost to empower
the church again. But the New Testament never teaches us to seek
this kind of experience.[5] We can no more repeat Pentecost than we
can reenact the crossing of the Red Sea or the feeding of the five
thousand. Like our own natural birth, this event marked the birth
of the church, and it need never be duplicated.

In fact, as a result of that first Pentecost, the Holy Spirit indwells
every believer at the moment of salvation—the moment of our own
spiritual birth (see 1 Cor. 6:19 and 12:13). Each of us has the
potential to be lionhearted witnesses for Christ. So rather than
another Pentecost experience, we simply need what Paul prayed
for—"to be strengthened with power through His Spirit in the inner
man" (Eph. 3:16b).

Denial

As a result of the Spirit's strength being demonstrated in Jerusalem that day, many understood the meaning of the gospel and
believed. However, others denied the miracle and scoffed at those
speaking in tongues.

Others were mocking and saying, "They are full of
sweet wine." (Acts 2:13)

"They are drunk!" This was the best explanation that some of
the people could offer of what they were hearing and seeing. But
how could drinking alcohol help one speak, with perfect inflection,
a previously unlearned language? Obviously, these dissenters were
just unwilling to recognize God's transforming power in the lives of
others. Even today, there are scoffers who may say to you, "This

5. In fact, the word Pentecost is only used twice more in the New Testament, both times as
a passing calendar reference: "Paul . . . was hurrying to be in Jerusalem, if possible, on the
day of Pentecost" (Acts 20:16), and, "I shall remain in Ephesus until Pentecost" (1 Cor. 16:8).

Christianity stuff, it's just a phase. It's just 'sweet wine.' You'll get over it when reality hits."

But when people are supernaturally transformed, it is the work of the sweet Spirit, not sweet wine. And it is real.

The Spirit's Coming . . . and Us Today

Skeptics may wag their heads, but when God touches a soul, a supernatural event takes place; a miracle happens. As a result, we can count on two principles being true.

First, *when God does a work, no one can duplicate or ignore the results.* Although we may try to change another person's life, only God has the ability to truly transform. In fact, if we step in too much, we may even trip up His efforts. But when His power does win out, the results are moving and amazing.

Second, *when the Spirit gives power, no one can deny or explain the change.* Skeptics may claim that such divine transformations can be explained naturally. But when the Spirit invades your heart, there is no natural rationale for your changed life. You are left with only one conclusion: something *super*natural has happened, and your life will never be the same.

☀ *Living Insights* STUDY ONE

God delights in touching our lives with unexpected moments of warmth. When He does this, things happen miraculously—that's the only way to describe it. Take a moment to read Craig Barnes' story of how God touched him when he was a lost and confused young man.

> After my parents got divorced and went their separate ways, my older brother and I spent a lot of time trying to figure out what had happened to our family. I was confused, hurt and furious at the turns life had taken. Eventually, I took to the road and began traveling around, trying to "find myself." But no matter how far I roamed, I couldn't escape the "why" questions. Why wasn't it working out at school? Why did I have no goals, no family and no future? And where in the world was God?

One Sunday afternoon I was hitchhiking some-where in Oklahoma. An older black couple pulled over in their battered pickup truck and offered me a ride. The driver introduced himself as Stanley Samuels. He told me that he and his wife were on their way to the Ebenezer Baptist Church, where he was a deacon. . . . Everybody always showed up for "Fifth Sunday—All Day Singing—Dinner on the Ground." They asked me to go with them. I started to say I was in a hurry, but the excuse sounded dumb before it even left my mouth.

As we made our way down the country road, Deacon Samuels and I got to know each other pretty well. He asked me what I was up to, and I told him I didn't have a clue. He told me that he had just lost his job at the cooperative grain mill, and he didn't really know why. Things were hard, but he really believed God knew that.

When we arrived . . . Deacon Samuels just walked around smiling, joking with friends. After a while I saw him stand tall and begin to hum "Amaz-ing Grace." By the time he got to the end of the first line, everyone had joined in singing, "I once was lost, but now am found. . . ."

I started to cry. It was the first time I'd cried since my mother had left. Now the tears wouldn't stop. They felt warm and reassuring.

. . . I learned a lot from Deacon Samuels that day, although he didn't give me a word of advice. . . .

. . . Through the fears, the pain and the hard questions, a glimmer of faith emerged, reminding me of the searching hands of the Father. I am found.[6]

Whether a lonely drifter or frazzled single parent, a travel-weary executive or love-hungry teenager, God's Spirit can find anyone, no matter how lost. Has He found you?

.

6. M. Craig Barnes, *Yearning: Living Between How It Is and How It Ought to Be* (Downers Grove, Ill.: InterVarsity Press, 1991), pp. 107–8.

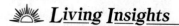

How has God's Spirit found you?

Recall an incident in which you were feeling lost, like the young man in the first Living Insight. Or maybe you were fearful and hiding, like the disciples in the Upper Room. In what way did the Holy Spirit move in your heart or in your circumstances so that you sensed God's love for you? Describe this situation and how it has changed your life. Then be like the disciples after the Spirit empowered them—share with another person what God has done for you.

_____

_____

_____

_____

_____

_____

_____

_____

_____

_____

_____

_____

_____

_____

_____

_____

_____

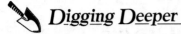 *Digging Deeper*

Some say that if the Holy Spirit is working in our lives, we should speak in tongues like the believers at Pentecost. Others teach that we should not speak in tongues. Which view is correct?

To help you decide your own position on this controversy, let's consider the following facts. Based on Acts 2, we can define tongues in its simplest form as "the ability to speak in a known language and dialect that has never been studied or learned, with the goal of rapidly disseminating the gospel into nations and cultures that have never heard about Christ."[7]

However, in 1 Corinthians there is evidence that another kind of tongues was practiced in the early church, because an interpreter was necessary to understand the message (1 Cor. 14:27–28). What is this other kind of tongues? Unfortunately, Paul does not precisely tell us.

We do know that in both Acts and 1 Corinthians, the purpose of tongues was evangelistic (Acts 2:8–11; 1 Cor. 14:20–22). The gift of tongues was a sign of God's power and presence to unbelievers while the church was being established.

The best way to evaluate the use of tongues today is by the guidelines in 1 Corinthians 14. Read Paul's instructions there carefully, and let the Spirit direct you concerning speaking in tongues.[8]

---

7. From the study guide *He Gave Gifts*, coauthored by Bryce Klabunde, from the Bible-teaching ministry of Charles R. Swindoll (Anaheim, Calif.: Insight for Living, 1992), pp. 72–73.

8. For further study on tongues, we recommend Insight for Living's *He Gave Gifts* study guide and J. Oswald Sanders' *The Holy Spirit and His Gifts*, rev. and enl. (Grand Rapids, Mich.: Zondervan Publishing House, 1970), pp. 123–35.

Chapter 5

PETER'S FIRST
SERMON . . . AND BEST
Acts 2:12–37

A young preacher stepped up to the pulpit of a little country church. This was his first sermon. Years of training and dreaming had finally been realized. He tried to look wise and pastoral, but he still couldn't keep his knees from knocking.

He straightened his well-rehearsed notes and opened his gold-edged graduation Bible. But before he could say, "Let's pray," a clatter arose at the back of the church. With a bang, the door sprang open and a herd of goats burst into the room.

His seminary professors had warned him about common sermon distractions: the occasional crying baby, the chronic latecomer, the note-passing teenager. But no one had told him about goats!

He tried to preach, but the goats were causing too much racket. So he took off his coat, rolled up his sleeves, and helped wrestle those goats out of the church. Being a shepherd of God's flock took on a whole new meaning for him that day. Needless to say, his first sermon was a disaster!

In Acts 2, another preacher—Peter—gave his first sermon. However, this sermon was his best, his most influential. It ignited a flame that would spread across continents and warm the world to the gospel of Christ. What made Peter's sermon so powerful? A review of the context in which he preached his message helps us understand its impact.

The Context of Peter's Sermon

We know that Peter's power did not come from himself. This fact is clear when we contrast this sermon with his words the night Jesus was arrested. Peter denied Christ then, saying, "I do not know Him" (see Luke 22:55–57). Now he courageously proclaims Him. What inspired his change of attitude?

The source of Peter's newfound courage is the Holy Spirit, who had invaded Peter's and the other believers' hearts in the Upper Room, miraculously empowering them to speak languages they had never learned (Acts 2:1–4). When the international crowds, who were in Jerusalem to celebrate Pentecost, heard Christ's emboldened followers, they were amazed and perplexed (vv. 5–12). And they were "saying to one another, 'What does this mean?'" (v. 12b).

Some in the audience accused them of being drunk (v. 13). At this point, Peter restrains himself no longer and rises to his feet. Without preparation or notes, he refutes the accusations and preaches a message that is a model for anyone who wants to communicate God's Word. What elements of his message make it so effective?

An Analysis of Peter's Sermon

First, his sermon is *simple.* Peter uses words everyone can understand. Even children can grasp the uncomplicated, nontechnical concepts he presents.

Second, his sermon is *scriptural.* Quoting from Joel and the Psalms, Peter constructs solid, biblical reasons to believe in Christ.

Third, his sermon is *Christ-centered.* The people's question, "What does this mean?" provides Peter a launching pad from which he fires off truths about Christ. Ultimately, these truths will transform the hearts of his listeners.

Peter shows us not only how to proclaim Christ's message but also what to say. Let's examine the content of Peter's sermon and learn how it can transform our lives as well.

The Content of Peter's Sermon

Amid the ruckus caused by the tongues miracle, Peter stands and proclaims,

> "Men of Judea, and all you who live in Jerusalem,
> let this be known to you, and give heed to my words."
> (v. 14b)

Capturing his audience, he proceeds with an explanation of what the baffling miracle means.

An Explanation of the Phenomenon

He first explains what the miracle is not. "These men are not drunk, as you suppose," he argues, "for it is only the third hour of the day" (v. 15). The third hour would have been 9:00 A.M., which in those days was too early to see someone drunk (1 Thess. 5:7).

37

No, alcohol hasn't overcome the believers. Something else has.

Then Peter explains what the miracle is—the fulfillment of prophecy.

> "This is what was spoken of through the prophet Joel:
> 'And it shall be in the last days,' God says,
> 'That I will pour forth of My Spirit upon all mankind;
> And your sons and your daughters shall prophesy,
> And your young men shall see visions,
> And your old men shall dream dreams;
> Even upon My bondslaves, both men and women,
> I will in those days pour forth of My Spirit
> And they shall prophesy.'"
> (Acts 2:16–18)

Centuries earlier, Joel foresaw a time when God would pour out His Spirit in a flood of grace and power.[1] "This," Peter tells the crowd, "is what you are now witnessing." Like an opening parenthesis, this pouring out of the Spirit signified the beginning of the age of grace.[2] And with a closing parenthesis, Joel's prophecy described the end of this era as well:

> "'And I will grant wonders in the sky above,
> And signs on the earth beneath,
> Blood, and fire, and vapor of smoke.
> The sun shall be turned into darkness,
> And the moon into blood,
> Before the great and glorious day of the Lord shall come.'"
> (vv. 19–20)

The Lord's cataclysmic return and judgment will mark the end of the age of grace. But in the period these new believers were

---

1. It is noteworthy that, although Peter is explaining the meaning of the tongues phenomenon, he doesn't even mention tongues in his sermon, only the pouring out of the Spirit.

2. A significant feature of this new age is that God gives His Spirit to all people who believe, Jew and Gentile. Thus, Gentiles "who formerly were far off have been brought near by the blood of Christ" (Eph. 2:13b).

entering and in which we now live, "everyone who calls on the name of the Lord shall be saved" (v. 21). Who is "the Lord?" What is this salvation?

As he continues, Peter paves a bloodstained path right to Calvary, the Cross, and Jesus—the heart of his sermon.

A Declaration of Christ

Building in intensity, Peter grabs hold of his audience again: "Men of Israel, listen to these words" (v. 22a). Then, as recorded in verses 22–36, he paints a stunning mural of Jesus, highlighting six truths about Him. The following chart summarizes these essential doctrines.

Six Doctrines about Christ (Acts 2:23–36)	
Incarnation	"Jesus the Nazarene, a man" (v. 22b)
Authentication	"attested to you by God with miracles and wonders and signs" (v. 22c)
Crucifixion	"this Man . . . you nailed to a cross . . . and put Him to death" (v. 23)
Resurrection[3]	"God raised Him up again" (v. 24)
Ascension[4]	"having been exalted to the right hand of God" (v. 33)
Glorification	"God has made Him both Lord and Christ" (v. 36)

Peter's portrait reveals every subtle detail of who Jesus Christ is as the Son of God. Skillfully drawing his point further, Peter reveals that it was this same Jesus who, "having received from the Father the promise of the Holy Spirit, . . . has poured forth this which you both see and hear" (v. 33). Jesus Himself is the One behind this tongues miracle.

---

3. Peter mentions the Resurrection twice, in verses 24 and 32. In between these two references, he quotes Psalm 16:8–11 as a prophecy verifying Jesus' resurrection (vv. 25–28). He explains that although David wrote this psalm centuries earlier, "he looked ahead and spoke of the resurrection of the Christ, that He was neither abandoned to Hades, nor did His flesh suffer decay" (v. 31).

4. Quoting Psalm 110:1, Peter verifies the Ascension with another prediction by David. "The Lord said to my Lord, 'Sit at My right hand, Until I make Thine enemies a footstool for Thy feet'" (Acts 2:34b–35).

Peter has now reached the climax of his sermon:

> "Therefore let all the house of Israel know for certain
> that God has made Him both Lord and Christ—this
> Jesus whom *you* crucified." (v. 36, emphasis added)

Guilty . . . with the slam of his gavel, Peter announces the verdict upon the crowd. Pierced to the heart, they respond with sincere repentance: "Brethren, what shall we do?" (v. 37).

A Personalization of Peter's Sermon

The people's question that day is the same one we ask when we feel the sting of sin's guilt. "What shall we do?" The answer may have surprised them then and may even surprise us today—believe in Christ. "Everyone who calls on the name of the Lord shall be saved" (v. 21).

Mere belief sounds too simple. Peter's audience was made up of "devout men" (v. 5), religious men who were dedicated to serving God. They wanted to know what they should *do*. Should they pray more, give more, work more?

Like them, maybe you have been religious all your life, committed to your church and helping others. Should you pray more, give more, work more for salvation? No . . . just believe in Christ.

> "Believe in the Lord Jesus, and you shall be saved."
> (16:31)

☀ *Living Insights*   STUDY ONE

Some religions are like an onion. Peel away layer upon layer of traditions and rules and programs and flash, and what do you have? Nothing. Their totals are just the sum of their layers.

True Christianity, on the other hand, is like a treasure chest. The outside may be unimpressive, but look inside and what do you find? A cross, an empty tomb, a promise of power, a hope of glory— riches beyond measure. And they're all embodied in one Person, Jesus.

What is your religious life like? Does it resemble an onion or a treasure chest? Explain why.

_____

_____

_____

_____

As W. H. Griffith Thomas once observed, "Christianity is nothing less and can be nothing more than relationship to Christ."[5] A relationship with Christ brings meaning to your religious involvements—as well as to every other area of your life. If Christ is absent from your life, you can start a relationship with Him today through simple faith. If you don't know how to express your trust in Christ, this prayer may help you put your desire into words:

> *Dear Jesus,*
>
> *I know my sins have come between us, and I stand as guilty as those who nailed you to the cross. But I believe that because of Your death and resurrection, You have put an end to the punishment and death I deserve. I trust in You for salvation and forgiveness—not in my own good works. Come into my heart. Be the center of my life. Empower me with Your Spirit. Amen.*[6]

Maybe you already have trusted in Christ for salvation, but your religion still feels onionlike. If this is true, perhaps you need to restore your relationship with Jesus. Are there some specific steps you can take to bring Him back into the center of your life? Record these steps in the space provided. Write from your heart, expressing your innermost desire for a close relationship with Him.

_____

_____

5. W. H. Griffith Thomas, *Christianity Is Christ* (London, England: Longmans, Green and Co., 1919), p. 7.

6. If through this prayer you have trusted Christ for salvation today, congratulations! Your decision draws you near to God as His precious child and seals your future in heaven (John 1:12; Eph. 1:13). Let us help you grow in your new faith. Please write our Counseling Department at Post Office Box 69000, Anaheim, California 92817-0900 for encouragement and information.

_____

_____

_____

_____

_____

_____

Have you ever tried explaining to someone what Christianity is? Here are a couple of ineffective ways some people have used:

- "Christianity is doing unto others what you would want them to do to . . . Or is it not doing unto others what you don't want them . . . ? I mean, it's doing unto others what you don't want them to . . . No, that's not it. It's . . . oh well, you know what I mean."

- "Christianity is not smoking, not drinking, not swearing, not going to parties, not getting angry, not going to movies, not watching too much TV, not dancing, not wearing your hair too long, not wearing your hair too short, and going to church."

Actually, Christianity is simple to define. It is *believing in Jesus Christ*. But what does a Christian believe about Jesus Christ? Peter's sermon in the lesson gives us the basics. In the blanks provided, write the name of the doctrine described. Please turn back to the chart in the lesson if you need help.

Who Is Jesus?   **Name of Doctrine**

Jesus is God who became a man . . .   _____

who proved His divinity by performing
miracles . . .   _____

who died on the cross, bearing the death
penalty for our sins . . .   _____

who was raised from the grave, conquering
death . . .   _____

who ascended to the right hand of God
the Father . . .   _____

who is exalted as Lord over all creation.   _____

Take some time to memorize these basic truths about Jesus. Knowing doctrine, though, is only part of understanding our faith. Ultimately, Christianity is a relationship with Christ. This means we

- talk to Him through prayer,
- represent Him by following His teachings,
- enjoy His love and guidance throughout life, and
- look forward to living in heaven with Him forever.

Only by knowing Jesus personally can you truly explain what Christianity is all about. In what ways can you develop your relationship with Christ this week?

_____

_____

_____

_____

_____

_____

_____

_____

_____

_____

Chapter 6

THE BIRTH
OF 3,000 BABIES

Acts 2:37–41

G od. The Almighty, the Lord of Hosts, the Great "I Am," the
Creator of the Universe, the Rock of Ages, the Proud Papa.
Proud Papa?

Perhaps you've never thought of God that way. But on the day
of Pentecost, when three thousand infant Christians were born, He
must have beamed with a joy to rival that of any new father.

In previous lessons, we visited the delivery room and witnessed
the beginning of the birth process—the gift of the Holy Spirit, the
miracle of tongues, and the curious throngs. Then Peter preached
his sermon and thousands believed in Jesus.

That's how the church entered the world . . . squinting,
stretching, and gazing up into the face of its smiling Papa. Let's go
back to that day and, for a few moments, relive the thrill of that
blessed event.

In Retrospect: The Declaration

In our last lesson, we focused on Peter's sermon. Before we
discuss what happened next, let's review three points.

Why It Was Preached

Peter delivered this message in response to the crowd that had
gathered. Thousands of people came out to investigate the noise
made when the Holy Spirit filled Christ's followers. When the newly
empowered Christians began speaking an assortment of foreign languages, some in the assemblage wondered what it meant (Acts
2:12b), and others thought they were drunk (v. 13). So Peter addressed those two issues.

What It Included

Peter began by explaining that the tongues miracle was motivated not by alcohol but by the Holy Spirit. It was a fulfillment of
Old Testament prophecy (vv. 14–21). Then he declared what Christ
was all about—crucified by the Jews, raised from the dead, and

ascended to the Father (vv. 22–36).

How Long It Took

Peter's sermon didn't take long to preach, probably less than four minutes. But it was impressively powerful. The Holy Spirit used his words to cause a heartfelt response in the audience.

In Response: The Question

Confronted with their wretched crime—the crucifixion of Christ—the people "were pierced to the heart" (v. 37b).[1]

Conviction of the Spirit

What was it about Peter's words that penetrated the people's armor and pricked their hearts? Hebrews 4:12–13 provides the answer:

> For the word of God is living and active and sharper than any two-edged sword, and piercing as far as the division of soul and spirit, of both joints and marrow, and able to judge the thoughts and intentions of the heart. And there is no creature hidden from His sight, but all things are open and laid bare to the eyes of Him with whom we have to do.

Like a razor-sharp, double-sided sword, the Scripture Peter quoted stabbed through the people's defenses, exposing their true nature. They could no longer hide, for they were guilty before God.

Reaction of the People

As a result, they cried out "to Peter and the rest of the apostles, 'Brethren, what shall we do?'" (Acts 2:37b).

Can you sense their anguish? Haven't you felt it, too, when sin's burden has crushed your spirit?

In Answer: The Explanation

Peter has a threefold answer to their question.

---

1. The Greek word for *pierce* is *katanussō*, which means "*to prick with a sharp point* . . . the puncture of a sharp . . . the sharp, painful emotion, the sting produced by Peter's word." Marvin R. Vincent, *Word Studies in the New Testament*, 2d ed. (McLean, Va.: MacDonald Publishing Co., n.d.), vol. 1, p. 455.

Repent!

First, Peter calls out for the people's repentance (v. 38a). When we hear the word *repent*, we often think it means feeling sorry for past behavior. But the Greek word carries a richer significance. Literally, it means "to change one's mind."[2] Peter exhorts the people to adopt an entirely different view about Christ.

They already feel bitter remorse for their sin, but that alone cannot save them. They need to go one step further and change what they believe. They must believe that Jesus is the Son of God and that His death and resurrection grant them new life. Thus, repentance and believing in Christ are really twin concepts (see Mark 1:15).

Be Baptized!

Second, Peter instructs the people to "be baptized in the name of Jesus Christ for the forgiveness of your sins" (Acts 2:38b). Some teachers use Peter's command to prove that baptism is necessary to receive God's forgiveness. But two small words in this verse guide us to a different interpretation. Let's look at the entire verse, emphasizing these key conjunctions:

> And Peter said to them, "Repent, *and* let each of you be baptized in the name of Jesus Christ *for* the forgiveness of your sins; and you shall receive the gift of the Holy Spirit." (v. 38, emphasis added)

The first word, *and*, implies a process: repent; then be baptized. Baptism is a response to repentance—an expression of faith. The second word, *for*, can mean "because of." Peter doesn't mean "be baptized so that you can receive forgiveness of sins."[3] Instead, he is saying, "be baptized because you have been forgiven of your sins." In this way, baptism illustrates spiritual cleansing. "Baptism is not the important thing here," contends Ray Stedman.

> It is repentance and belief in His name that obtains remission of sins. It is changing your mind about

2. Gerhard Kittel, ed., *Theological Dictionary of the New Testament*, trans. and ed. Geoffrey W. Bromiley (1967; reprint, Grand Rapids, Mich.: William B. Eerdmans Publishing Co., 1973), vol. 4, p. 976.

3. For further proof that this is what Peter means, see Acts 10:43, where he addresses another crowd. He gives similar salvation instructions, but omits the baptism requirement: "Everyone who believes in Him receives forgiveness of sins."

Jesus Christ that enables God to wipe out all your guilt and all the sins of your past.[4]

When we receive Christ, God wipes out our guilt and sin. What a promise!

> "For the promise is for you and your children, and for all who are far off, as many as the Lord our God shall call to Himself." (v. 39)

Before we come to know Him, a choking mustiness of guilt blankets us all. But because of our faith, God, in His mercy, lets in a cool breath of air—the grace of His forgiveness.

Be Saved!

Finally, the Apostle urges his listeners to "be saved from this perverse generation!" (v. 40b). We know from the original Greek that his appeal is passionate: "Be saved from this generation—this perverse one!"[5]

Why was Peter's plea so emphatic? Because he knew the destructive impact of that society's valueless lifestyle. He desired that the believers be saved not just from hell's fires but from the world's volatile influence as well.

Do we live in a "perverse" generation today? A five-minute read of the morning newspaper or even a twenty-second glance at the television awakens us to the crookedness of our world. Its wayward morals can suffocate anyone who wanders onto its path—unbeliever or believer. Surely we know some of our sinful society's effects: fear, loneliness, depression, addictions, and strife. We need to be delivered, to be freed from these things. But how?

We can be saved from the twisted, tangled way of the world by following the straight path God has set for us in Scripture, empowered for the journey by the Spirit who was given to us when we first believed.

---

4. Ray Stedman, *Acts 1–12: Birth of the Body* (Santa Ana, Calif.: Vision House Publishers, 1974), p. 57.

5. The Greek word for *perverse* is *skolios*, from which we derive our word *scoliosis*, meaning "an abnormal curvature of the spine." In Greek, the word means "'winding,' 'twisted,' 'tortuous,' 'slanting' and in a ... sense 'crooked,' 'dishonest,' 'unfair.' " Gerhard Friedrich, ed., *Theological Dictionary of the New Testament*, trans. and ed. Geoffrey W. Bromiley (Grand Rapids, Mich.: William B. Eerdmans Publishing Co., 1971), vol. 7, p. 403.

In Application: The Appropriation

The people's response to Peter's threefold plea for repentance, baptism, and salvation must have thrilled him and the other disciples. Individually, "those who had received his word were baptized" (v. 41a). And collectively, when all the heads were counted, "there were added that day about three thousand souls" (v. 41b).

When that day had dawned, a roomful of faithful but powerless followers of Christ sat together, praying and waiting. By the time the sun had set, thousands more carried the flame of God's Spirit in their hearts. In them new life had begun.

The church was born.

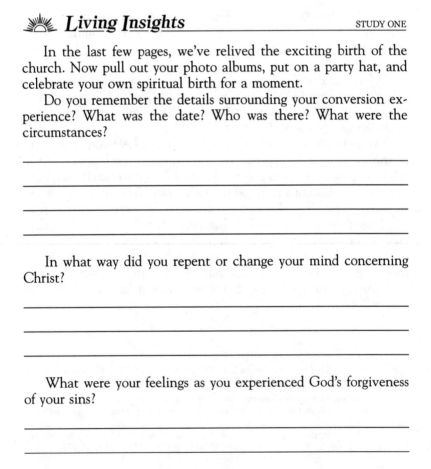

🌅 Living Insights

In the last few pages, we've relived the exciting birth of the church. Now pull out your photo albums, put on a party hat, and celebrate your own spiritual birth for a moment.

Do you remember the details surrounding your conversion experience? What was the date? Who was there? What were the circumstances?

_____

_____

_____

_____

In what way did you repent or change your mind concerning Christ?

_____

_____

_____

What were your feelings as you experienced God's forgiveness of your sins?

_____

_____

How have you observed the power of the Holy Spirit in your life since you became a Christian?

_____

_____

_____

Following your conversion, were you baptized? If so, describe it, including your thoughts and emotions.

_____

_____

_____

How has following Christ's straight path since you believed in Him saved you from the world's crooked and dangerous path?

_____

_____

_____

Have you ever been asked to give your testimony but refrained because you didn't know what to say? Now you no longer have that excuse because you've just written it down. Share your testimony with someone soon. And leave the party hat on—it becomes you!

🌅 *Living Insights* STUDY TWO

What does God's forgiveness feel like? Max Lucado's story of Maria and her teenage daughter Christina helps us understand.

The story takes place in Brazil. Christina is tired of life in the dusty village and longs for the excitement of the big city. One morning her mother finds her bed empty . . .

> Maria knew immediately where her daughter had gone. She also knew immediately what she must do

49

to find her. She quickly threw some clothes in a bag, gathered up all her money, and ran out of the house.

On her way to the bus stop she entered a drugstore to get one last thing. Pictures. She sat in the photograph booth, closed the curtain, and spent all she could on pictures of herself. With her purse full of small black-and-white photos, she boarded the next bus to Rio de Janeiro.

Maria knew Christina had no way of earning money. She also knew that her daughter was too stubborn to give up. When pride meets hunger, a human will do things that were before unthinkable. Knowing this, Maria began her search. Bars, hotels, nightclubs, any place with the reputation for street walkers or prostitutes. She went to them all. And at each place she left her picture—taped on a bathroom mirror, tacked to a hotel bulletin board, fastened to a corner phone booth. . . .

It wasn't too long before both the money and the pictures ran out, and Maria had to go home. The weary mother wept as the bus began its long journey back to her small village.

It was a few weeks later that young Christina descended the hotel stairs. Her young face was tired. Her brown eyes no longer danced with youth but spoke of pain and fear. Her laughter was broken. Her dream had become a nightmare. A thousand times over she had longed to trade these countless beds for her secure pallet. Yet the little village was, in too many ways, too far away.

As she reached the bottom of the stairs, her eyes noticed a familiar face. She looked again, and there on the lobby mirror was a small picture of her mother. Christina's eyes burned and her throat tightened as she walked across the room and removed the small photo. Written on the back was this compelling invitation. "Whatever you have done, whatever you have become, it doesn't matter. Please come home."

She did.[6]

What does God's forgiveness feel like? It feels like coming home. If you need the Lord's forgiveness but have been too proud or too afraid, take a few moments to express your need to Him. Make this time your own special homecoming.

_____

_____

_____

_____

_____

_____

_____

_____

_____

_____

_____

_____

_____

_____

_____

_____

_____

6. Max Lucado, No Wonder They Call Him the Savior (Portland, Oreg.: Multnomah Press, 1986), pp. 158–59.

Chapter 7

SPIRITUAL PEDIATRICS

Acts 2:41–47

N ow what do we do?" he whispers.

The young father turns to his wife, and they both look down at the sleeping newborn they've just brought home from the hospital. They've arranged the nursery just right, read the latest parenting theories, and stocked two closets full of baby gadgets. However, none of this preparation can answer his question or equip them for the road ahead. Late night feedings, endless diapering, and constant doctor visits fill the immediate horizon. And in the years to come, they'll have to contend with temper tantrums, little white lies, and fits of nose-thumbing defiance. For these young parents, "Now what do we do?" is an excellent question.

As the apostles surveyed the thousands of baby believers who had joined the church on the Day of Pentecost, they must have asked that same question. These newborn Christians would require wise parenting to learn how to walk with Christ, handle temptation, worship, and pray. The apostles, however, had no instruction manual to follow—no Bible, no handbooks, no guidelines. How would they nurture these young ones? How would the infant church survive and grow?

When the excitement of spiritual birth gave way to the reality of day-to-day life, the leaders did do something. They rolled up their sleeves and began caring for all these spiritual babies. As a result, the church thrived. How did the apostles parent these newest members of God's family? That's the topic of our lesson today.

Setting the Scene

After the Day of Pentecost, Jerusalem resembled a spiritual nursery. Luke summarizes the situation:

> So then, those who had received his word were baptized; and there were added that day about three thousand souls. (Acts 2:41)

They "received his word"—in other words, they accepted Peter's gospel message and were saved. They then declared their salvation through baptism, and three thousand were "added." To what were they added?

They were added to the church (see also v. 47). Unlike a church building with pews and a pulpit, God's universal church is a family. God designed His church to provide protection, nourishment, and growth for its members through family relationships. In this way, the church is a spiritual incubator, providing warmth and encouragement for new believers.

Within this environment, the apostles nursed the infant Christians by emphasizing four activities. These priorities became the church's lifeblood and have become essential aspects of today's church as well.

Priorities of the People

We know that these activities were priorities in the early church because, according to Acts 2:42, the Christians were continually devoting themselves to them.[1] What were they? Take a look at the rest of this verse:

> They were continually devoting themselves to the apostles' teaching and to fellowship, to the breaking of bread and to prayer.

Teaching

Their first priority was to the teaching. The apostles were the instructors, and though we aren't sure what they taught, they probably used the Old Testament Scriptures along with the words of Christ to feed the people.

Their work as spiritual pediatricians undoubtedly began with nourishment on God's Word. Sound teaching for new believers then and now is like milk to a baby. A diet that neglects the Bible develops weak Christians unable to handle temptations or trials. Instead, as Peter commands,

> Like newborn babes, long for the pure milk of the word, that by it you may grow in respect to salvation. (1 Pet. 2:2)

1. "The verb translated 'devoted' (*proskartereō*) is a common one that connotes a steadfast and singleminded fidelity to a certain course of action." Richard N. Longenecker, "The Acts of the Apostles," in *The Expositor's Bible Commentary*, ed. Frank E. Gaebelein (Grand Rapids, Mich.: Zondervan Publishing House, Regency Reference Library, 1981), vol. 9, p. 289.

Fellowship

The second priority was fellowship. *Koinōnia* is the Greek word for *fellowship* in verse 42, and it comes from a root word that means "common."[2] The early Christians shared a commonality with one another based on their faith in Christ. Their *koinōnia* manifested itself in two ways: they shared *in* their common experiences of joy and sorrow, and they shared *with* one another material gifts and words of love and encouragement.

Their fellowship was an expression of vibrant, authentic Christianity in action. We can taste that same kind of sweet fellowship in our churches today; but, as Anne Ortlund writes, it is a choice.

> Every congregation has a choice to be one of two things. You can choose to be a bag of marbles, single units that don't affect each other except in collision. On Sunday morning you can choose to go to church or to sleep in: who really cares whether there are 192 or 193 marbles in a bag?
>
> Or you can choose to be a bag of grapes. The juices begin to mingle, and there is no way to extricate yourselves if you tried. Each is part of all.[3]

Communion

The third activity to which the early believers were continually devoting themselves was "the breaking of bread." This was more than eating meals together. They also celebrated the Lord's Supper, just as Christ had asked all His followers to do (see Luke 22:19).[4]

By regularly taking communion, they kept their minds and hearts focused on Christ. This focus is indispensable in our walk with the Lord. Worshiping at the Lord's Table is spiritual therapy for our burdened souls. Like a warm home after a difficult day, it surrounds us with Christ's love and restores our sense of purpose.

How did they celebrate the Lord's Supper? With crackers and

---

2. "*Koinōnia* (from *koinos*, 'common') bears witness to the common life of the church in two senses. First, it expresses what we share in together. . . . But secondly, *koinōnia* also expresses what we share out together, what we give as well as what we receive." John Stott, *The Spirit, the Church, and the World* (Downers Grove, Ill.: InterVarsity Press, 1990), pp. 82–83.

3. Anne Ortlund, *Up with Worship* (Glendale, Calif.: Regal Books, A Division of G/L Publications, 1975), p. 67.

4. The early Christians practiced baptism (v. 41) and the Lord's Supper. These two activities are known as the ordinances of the church.

juice, or bread and wine? Was it somber and reflective, or joyous and uplifting? Acts 2:46 simply says they were "breaking bread from house to house." The lack of any further specifics gives us freedom concerning when, where, and how we take communion. What is important is the meaning of the ceremony, that we honor Christ for His body that was broken and for His blood that was spilled for us.

Prayer

Finally, they emphasized prayer. The Greek says literally "they were continually devoting themselves to *the prayers*" (v. 42). It implies that this was standard practice when they met together. Their prayers were a priority because through them they kindled a personal involvement with one another and sparked a desire to serve the Lord. They listened to and cared for each other in the most profound way—by praying for each other.

We also can experience this same kindling effect when we pray with other believers. When we choose to isolate ourselves, we become like a charred ember that falls from the fire, cold and dark inside. But when we join with others in prayer, we glow with an enthusiasm to serve the Lord and reflect His radiance.

By making these four activities top priorities, the apostles nurtured the young Christians with the intensive care they needed to grow into mature adults. Were they successful? Yes, through the power of the Holy Spirit. Verses 43–46 describe the results.

Amplification of the Activities

Relating back to the four priorities in verse 42, Luke expands on the results of each activity. First, we see what happened in the people's hearts when they absorbed the apostles' teaching.

As They Were Instructed . . .

Everyone kept feeling a sense of awe; and many wonders and signs were taking place through the apostles. (v. 43)

The truths taught by the apostles rumbled like thunder from heaven, filling the people with awe. *Phobos* is the Greek word translated *awe*, meaning a "reverential fear."[5] These early believers came

5. G. Abbott-Smith, *A Manual Greek Lexicon of the New Testament* (Edinburgh, Scotland: T. & T. Clark, 1937), p. 472.

face-to-face with God and His Word, and as a result, a reverence for His power and majesty enveloped the entire church.

Teachers like the apostles, who reveal God in His awe-inspiring glory, are never frightening or manipulative. They simply pull back the curtain of heaven so that we catch just a glimmer of God's brilliance. When we do, we have no other response than that of Isaiah, who saw the Lord and said,

> Woe is me, for I am ruined!
> Because I am a man of unclean lips,
> And I live among a people of unclean lips;
> For my eyes have seen the King, the Lord of hosts.
> (Isa. 6:5)

When the apostles taught God's truth, the people not only felt awe but also witnessed signs and wonders. Through these miracles, God validated the apostles' authority.

As They Experienced Koinōnia . . .

> All those who had believed were together, and had all things in common; and they began selling their property and possessions, and were sharing them with all, as anyone might have need. (Acts 2:44–45)

Christ's love brimmed in the people's hearts and overflowed into unity, selflessness, and concern for one another—even to the point of selling their own property to help those in need. This kind of giving and fellowship cannot be injected into a group externally; it must come from within. And it can only be fostered in an environment that encourages freedom and openness, a place where there is koinōnia.

As They Ate Together . . .

> Day by day continuing with one mind in the temple, and breaking bread from house to house, they were taking their meals together with gladness and sincerity of heart. (v. 46)

We often associate the Lord's Supper with quiet contemplation, but this verse describes the event as a time for gladness, joy, even laughter. In the same breath, Luke also says it produced a "sincerity of heart." The word sincerity in Greek comes from a root word that

56

literally means "free from rock" or "smooth,"[6] implying that their meetings were free from contentiousness—there were no emotional rough edges. This kind of atmosphere makes for good cheer and harmony, delightful results of a meaningful communion experience.

Finally, the early church's prayers produced equally significant results.

As They Continued in Prayer . . .

[They were] praising God, and having favor with all the people. And the Lord was adding to their number day by day those who were being saved. (v. 47)

Their prayers built two bridges: one vertically to the Lord and one horizontally to each other. By praising the Lord, the people turned their attention on God and His power; and by loving one another, they brought unity to the church. As a result, the church grew.

Growth occurred because the apostles nurtured the church through these four priorities. Are they priorities in your church? In your family? In your life?

Response of the Reader

As you seek to incorporate teaching, fellowship, the Lord's Supper, and prayer in your life, consider the following two principles. They capsulize the apostles' spiritual nutrition plan for us.

First, *the healthy Christian is a balanced believer.* The apostles' activities were like the four basic food groups to the early church. Instruction was balanced with involvement, beliefs with behavior, the vertical relationship with the horizontal, and a fear of the Lord with fellowship with others. Because the young believers ate equally from all four, healthy development occurred. Growth will take place in our lives as well when we follow this balanced spiritual diet.

Second, *authentic Christianity brings happiness and harmony.* Childish behavior is marked by moodiness, selfishness, and petty arguments. But mature attitudes bring harmony and cooperation. The same is true in the spiritual realm. Mature Christians know authentic joy in spite of their circumstances because they have grown up on a steady intake of the staples of the Christian life.

6. Archibald Thomas Robertson, *Word Pictures in the New Testament* (Grand Rapids, Mich.: Baker Book House, 1930), vol. 3, p. 40.

Use the following chart as a mirror to reflect how well you're balancing the four priorities we discussed in the lesson. Under each category, jot down the various activities in which you are involved. Under the "Lord's Supper," include activities that involve other types of worship as well, such as Sunday morning services.

Teaching	*Fellowship*
Lord's Supper/Worship	*Group Prayer*

Do you see any area that is over- or underemphasized? Which is it? How do you think you can bring this priority back into balance with the others?

_____

_____

_____

Maybe your chart is so full that each area overwhelms you. If so, how can you restructure your involvements to include more family or personal time?

_____

_____

_____

Maybe your chart is sparsely filled. If this is true, how can you add to your involvements in each area? Remember to start slow and stay balanced, possibly adding just one activity per category.

_____

_____

_____

☀ *Living Insights* STUDY TWO

After the thrill of witnessing a spiritual birth, the hard work begins. Based on the apostles' example in our lesson, what parenting qualities would you suppose are important for someone spiritually guiding a young believer?

_____

_____

_____

According to the following verses, how will the spiritual parent know if a young believer has grown to maturity?

Hebrews 5:14 _____

2 Timothy 2:2 _____

Ephesians 4:13–15 _____

Do you feel that God has given you the qualities and vision needed to spiritually parent a younger believer? If so, whom has He placed on your heart? How can you begin caring for this person soon?

_____

_____

_____

Chapter 8

THE CRIPPLE WHO DANCED IN CHURCH
Acts 3:1–26

Beat the odds! Never say die! Soar like an eagle!

These are mottos of people who rise above life's difficulties to fulfill their dreams. Some do this through sheer hard work and determination. For example, Booker T. Washington, who was born a slave, desired an education in spite of his family's desperate poverty. After much effort and study, he graduated from college, became the president of Tuskegee Institute, and is now considered to be "the most influential spokesman for black Americans" of his day.[1]

Others overcome their disadvantages through creativity. One man employed his imagination in solving a Goliath-sized problem when developers built a gleaming supermarket and a gigantic discount house on either side of his tiny general store. Undaunted, he scraped together his savings and purchased an eye-catching neon sign. Placed right over his storefront between the two mammoth competitors, it read: Main Entrance Here![2]

Sometimes, however, no matter how much hard work, no matter how much creativity, the odds are unbeatable. Such is the case in the following passage. We will meet a man lame from birth, an outcast who survives by begging. It would take an act of God to heal him of his disadvantage.

Miracle of Healing

Chapter 2 of Acts concludes in triumph, describing the heavenly ideal of people praising God and loving one another. Chapter 3 brings us back to earth, opening with the image of the pitiful lame man begging for alms.

---

1. *The New Encyclopaedia Britannica*, 15th ed., see "Washington, Booker T."

2. Dale E. Galloway, *Rebuild Your Life* (Wheaton, Ill.: Tyndale House Publishers, 1987), pp. 116–17.

Setting

> Now Peter and John were going up to the temple
> at the ninth hour, the hour of prayer. And a certain
> man who had been lame from his mother's womb
> was being carried along, whom they used to set down
> every day at the gate of the temple which is called
> Beautiful, in order to beg alms of those who were
> entering the temple. (vv. 1–2)

The scene takes place at the temple. The time is 3:00 P.M., the hour for the Jews to gather and pray. Among those who come are Peter and John, two well-known leaders of a burgeoning religious movement.

In contrast to their importance, an unknown paralytic sits with his hand outstretched, hoping to spark pity in any passerby. Today, like every other day, he has been carried here and placed on his spot to beg for money.

Put yourself in his filthy beggar's rags . . . can you feel his despair? He can go nowhere without help; he relies completely on others' handouts; his only purpose in living is survival. Being an invalid since birth, he has never known a healthy day, has never stretched out his legs and walked to the market or to a friend's house. Instead, his legs are useless appendages—two perpetual reminders of the lifelessness he feels deep within his soul.

Discussing

"Alms . . . alms . . . ," he says, trying to catch someone's eye. In the afternoon rush, a mix of people shuffle by him, but he notices two who seem different.

> And when he saw Peter and John about to go into
> the temple, he began asking to receive alms. And
> Peter, along with John, fixed his gaze upon him and
> said, "Look at us!" And he began to give them his
> attention, expecting to receive something from
> them. (vv. 3–5)

What does he expect from the two men? He expects money. Instead, Peter's next words address the man's innermost yearning, his for deeper need

> "I do not possess silver and gold, but what I do have

61

I give to you: In the name of Jesus Christ the Nazarene—*walk!*" (v. 6, emphasis added)

Healing

"Wha . . .?" The lame man doesn't even have time to object, for Peter has grasped for his begging hand.

> And seizing him by the right hand, he raised him up; and immediately his feet and his ankles were strengthened. And with a leap, he stood upright and began to walk; and he entered the temple with them, walking and leaping and praising God. (vv. 7–8)

In the time it takes him to stand up, the man's tendons attach, his muscles grow, and his sockets realign. Life fills his legs! "The lame will leap like a deer," Isaiah once predicted (35:6a). And like a deer this man leaps, bursting with the pleasure of God.

Praising

Together they enter the temple. None praise God more exuberantly this day than Peter, John, and, especially, the healed man, who jumps and dances in joy and worship. Soon heads begin to turn . . .

> And all the people saw him walking and praising God; and they were taking note of him as being the one who used to sit at the Beautiful Gate of the temple to beg alms, and they were filled with wonder and amazement at what had happened to him. (Acts 2:9–10)

Message of Hope

A shock wave of whispers, gasps, and stares spreads through the temple. Amazed onlookers crowd around, and the healed man clings to the apostles like a baby animal to his mother (v. 11).

Explanation: Power Is from God, Not Man

Who caused this miracle? What does it mean? The people's thoughts immediately focus on Peter and John. But Peter speaks up, shining the spotlight on Christ.

"Men of Israel, why do you marvel at this, or why

do you gaze at us, as if by our own power or piety we had made him walk? The God of Abraham, Isaac, and Jacob, the God of our fathers, has glorified His servant Jesus." (vv. 12b–13a)

Jesus is the One who performed this miracle; Peter claims none of the credit. Instead, he uses the opportunity to explain who Jesus is and the nature of true faith.

Declaration: Faith Is through Christ, Not Self

Taking a moment to refresh the people's memory, Peter reminds them that Jesus was the One whom they had "delivered up, and disowned in the presence of Pilate, when he had decided to release Him" (v. 13b). They had "disowned the Holy and Righteous One, and asked for a murderer," Barabbas (v. 14). They had even "put to death the Prince of life, the one whom God raised from the dead" (v. 15).

Isolating the subject of faith, Peter continues:

> "And on the basis of faith in His name, it is the name of Jesus which has strengthened this man whom you see and know; and the faith which comes *through Him* has given him this perfect health in the presence of you all." (v. 16, emphasis added)

The man was healed by the authority of Jesus' name—the Prince of Life. Even the faith shown by Peter and the man came from Christ. They did not empower the miracle; Christ did, according to His sovereign will. Peter simply submitted himself to Christ's will and acted on what he believed, and the man was healed.

In this way, Christ's life-giving power restored dead limbs. And it also began to revive spiritually lifeless hearts.

Invitation: Hope Is in Heaven, Not Earth

Peter turns the healing of the lame man into an object lesson of a higher truth, the gospel.

> "And now, brethren, I know that you acted in ignorance, just as your rulers did also. But the things which God announced beforehand by the mouth of all the prophets, that His Christ should suffer, He has thus fulfilled. Repent therefore and return, that your sins may be wiped away, in order that times of

63

refreshing may come from the presence of the Lord; and that He may send Jesus, the Christ appointed for you." (vv. 17–20)

What will happen if the people repent and believe in Christ? Peter says that, first, their sins will be completely forgiven. Second, refreshment will wash over their weary souls. And third, Jesus will come to live within them.

Like the beggar, the people bear their burdens alone. But if they believe, Christ will be their constant companion, freeing them from sin. With Christ, their refreshed spirits will leap with joy, praising God. They can overcome sin's disadvantage, not by hard work, not by creative thinking, but by Christ's power.

Meaning of Health

As the once-lame man clung to Peter and John, listening to the truth of the gospel, what was he thinking? Looking out on the crowd, did he not see the faces of so many who had walked past him day after day? Once he envied their health and vitality. Now he pities them. They are the true paralytics, for they are lame of heart.

Have you been living spiritually disadvantaged? Have you felt purposeless and emotionally paralyzed? Do you need Christ's touch to invigorate your soul? If so, keep in mind these two principles of good inner health.

First, *enjoy periodic times of refreshing.* By trusting Christ, you'll experience refreshment. Think of it as a revolving door: out goes discouragement, in comes hope; out goes pain, in comes joy. This refreshment may come through a meaningful song, a poignant sermon, an embrace by a friend, or the Word of God. When it comes, you'll know it is from Christ.

Second, *live each day under the blessing of God, drawing moment by moment upon His power.* The Holy Spirit's power is strong enough to heal our gravest disappointments and mend our deepest fears. And when we daily turn ourselves over to Christ, blemishes and all, He will transform us into new people. Through Him we *can* soar like eagles!

> Yet those who wait for the Lord
> Will gain new strength;
> They will mount up with wings like eagles,

They will run and not get tired,
They will walk and not become weary.
(Isa. 40:31)

☀ *Living Insights*

Whatever your disadvantage—physical, emotional, or spiritual —God's grace is sufficient. This means that God, through His grace, has the power to turn your disadvantage into His advantage. How can He do that?

Let's examine 2 Corinthians 12:9–10 to answer this question. In verse 9, what advantage does Paul ascribe to his weakness?

_____

_____

In verse 10, Paul says that he is "content." How can he be content in the face of "weaknesses . . . insults . . . distresses . . . persecutions . . . difficulties"?

_____

_____

Knowing that Christ's power will emanate out of our inadequacies, we can face today with hope. We can have what Joni Eareckson Tada calls "present-tense faith."

It's taking God's promises and acting on them *today.* This "right now" way of looking at God's assurances is the stuff of which great people of faith are made. They simply take God at His Word and live on that basis. . . .

When I started living like this, I suddenly understood I could get a jump-start on heaven. I could start living for eternity today. I could have confidence that God had His busy fingers working on me moment by moment, even though I couldn't see or feel them.

Great faith isn't the ability to believe long and far into the misty future. It's simply taking God at

His word and taking the next step.[3]

Do you have this kind of faith? Are you trusting in God's gracious power through your disadvantage? What do you need to do to take "the next step"?

_____

_____

_____

_____

☀ *Living Insights* STUDY TWO

In what ways has God healed you . . .

physically? _____

_____

emotionally? _____

_____

spiritually? _____

_____

The healed man's first steps were leaps of joy and praise. Like David, who danced "before the Lord with all his might" (2 Sam. 6:14a), this man freely worshiped God.

How can you praise the Lord for His many healings in your life? You may not choose to leap for joy in a church service, but what creative ways can you think of to express your gratitude to Him?

_____

_____

_____

---

3. Joni Eareckson Tada, *Glorious Intruder* (Portland, Oreg.: Multnomah, 1989), pp. 27–28.

Praise the Lord, O my soul.
I will praise the Lord all my life;
I will sing praise to my God as long as I live.
(Ps. 146:1b–2, NIV).

 ## Digging Deeper

Peter's healing of the lame man gives us a measure by which we can evaluate faith-healing ministries today.

1. *When God heals, it is immediate.* The lame man's feet and ankles were immediately strengthened.

2. *When God heals, it is supernatural.* The man's muscles were atrophied and his joints had cemented. God miraculously developed new tendons and sockets because they couldn't mend naturally.

3. *When God heals, it is perfect.* The lame man was given perfect health. He felt no more pain or recurring weakness in his legs.

4. *When God heals, it is according to His will.* God chose to heal this one lame man among all the disabled in Jerusalem.

5. *When God heals, it is not ultimately dependent on man's faith.* The lame man did not expect or seek healing. Jesus, too, healed people despite their lack of faith (Mark 9:14–29).

6. *When God heals, it always brings glory to Christ.* Peter never took the credit for his gift of healing.

7. *When God heals, it is for a purpose.* The healing was not the end but the means to proclaiming and authenticating the gospel.[4]

4. For further information on miracles and healing, see the study guide He Gave Gifts, coauthored by Bryce Klabunde, from the Bible-teaching ministry of Charles R. Swindoll (Anaheim, Calif.: Insight for Living, 1992).

Chapter 9

RELIGION VERSUS CHRISTIANITY

Acts 4:1–22

The greatest adversary to Christianity is religion. Surprised? It's true.

Every religion has one basic characteristic. Its followers are trying to reach God, find God, please God through their own efforts. Religions reach up toward God. Christianity is God reaching down to man. Christianity claims that men have not found God, but that God has found them.[1]

. . . *reach God*

. . . *find God*

. . . *please God*

Religion cringes at this thought. It insists that we try to be good enough to win God's favor. It puts us on a treadmill, laboring to win His approval, but resulting in frustration and failure. Religion can even become hostile when we oppose its sys-

1. Fritz Ridenour, *How to Be a Christian without Being Religious* (Glendale, Calif.: G/L Publications, Regal Books, 1967), introduction.

tem. In Christ's day, it scoffed at Christ's claim of deity. It trembled with rage when He said that sin blocks our way to God. It clenched its fists when Christ's followers preached that He was the only bridge to eternal life. Then, when it was faced with the freedom Jesus Christ provides, legalistic religion was ready to fight.

In this lesson, we'll witness such a fight as some religious moguls square off against Peter, John, and their newest convert, the lame man who was healed by the power of Jesus.

The Clash: Enter Religion

Since the Holy Spirit's arrival on the Day of Pentecost, Christianity had been winning the hearts of the people. This was happening right under the noses of the religious leaders, who thought they had rid themselves of the "troublemaker," Jesus, when they crucified Him. Then a certain event occurred that left them wondering whether Jesus was dead and buried after all.

Main Event and Major Characters

Performing a miracle typical of Jesus, Peter healed a man who had been lame since birth. Then he began preaching the gospel of Christ in the temple—in full view of the religious leaders. How did these watchdogs of the temple react?

> And as they were speaking to the people, the priests and the captain of the temple guard, and the Sadducees, came upon them, being greatly disturbed because they were teaching the people and proclaiming in Jesus the resurrection from the dead. (Acts 4:1–2)

Among those leaders disturbed by Peter's message were the Sadducees. A quick look at who they were will give us insight into why Peter riled them so.

> They were the ruling class of wealthy aristocrats. Politically, they ingratiated themselves with the Romans, and followed a policy of collaboration, so that they feared the subversive implications of the apostles' teaching. Theologically, they . . . denied the doctrine of the resurrection of the dead, which the apostles proclaimed in Jesus. . . . They thus saw the

apostles as both agitators and heretics, both disturbers of the peace and enemies of truth.[2]

Complaint and Consequences

By teaching that Jesus rose from the dead, Peter was stirring up the religious waters. His message threatened the Sadducees' faulty beliefs as well as their position in society. Consequently,

> they laid hands on them, and put them in jail until the next day, for it was already evening. (v. 3)

This was the first persecution of the church, a precursor to countless imprisonments and mistreatments of Christians throughout history. But then, as now, when the oppressors locked up the messengers, they unleashed the message even more. As a result, the church grew unabatedly.

> Many of those who had heard the message believed; and the number of the men came to be about five thousand. (v. 4)

The Inquisition: Religion Exposed

The apostles' trial took place the next day, and all the religious heavyweights gathered to take a swipe at Peter and John. Their tactics expose three characteristics of how religion operates when it takes the offensive against Christianity.

Its Characteristics

When threatened, religion exercises intimidation. With great pomp, the "rulers and elders and scribes" (v. 5) assembled to give their opinions of Peter and John. Religion finds security in numbers, in formalism, and in status, using these class barriers to intimidate and manipulate.

When uncertain, religion emphasizes tradition. Among the dignitaries present were "Annas the high priest . . . and Caiaphas and John and Alexander, and all who were of high-priestly descent" (v. 6). These men could trace their roots back to the high priests of early Israel.

2. John Stott, *The Spirit, the Church, and the World* (Downers Grove, Ill.: InterVarsity Press, 1990), p. 95.

The assembly Luke describes here is the Sanhedrin, the Supreme Court of the Jews. This venerated body had its origins in Old Testament times, when Moses called together seventy men to help him adjudicate matters in Israel (Num. 11:16). Through the centuries, this court wrote the final word concerning civil and religious law, and during the time of Jesus and the apostles, "the Sanhedrin came to possess the greatest power and jurisdiction of its history."[3]

Entrenched in tradition, this group frowned on new teaching. They considered themselves the interpreters and keepers of ancient truth; and when Peter and John challenged them, they burrowed deeper into their ways, unwilling to budge.

When suspicious, religion employs interrogation. Gathered in a semicircle, they placed Peter, John, and the healed man in the center and fired menacing questions at them: "By what power, or in what name, have you done this?" (Acts 4:7b).

Normally, the pressures of intimidation, tradition, and interrogation would unhinge anybody. But not Peter. How could he be so confident, standing before seventy of the most powerful men of his day? Because he recognized that, no matter how portentous, religion had its limitations. It would always bow to the truth of Christ.

Its Limitations

The first limitation Peter recognized was that *religion lacks the Spirit's filling.* Peter had tapped into a power source the religious leaders lacked, for he was "filled with the Holy Spirit" (v. 8a). He stood his ground and spoke the truth courageously:

> "Rulers and elders of the people, if we are on trial today for a benefit done to a sick man, as to how this man has been made well, let it be known to all of you, and to all the people of Israel, that by the name of Jesus Christ the Nazarene, whom you crucified, whom God raised from the dead—by this name this man stands here before you in good health. He is the stone which was rejected by you, the builders, but which became the very corner stone." (vv. 8b–11)

3. D. A. Hagner, "Sanhedrin," The Zondervan Pictorial Encyclopedia of the Bible, ed. Merrill C. Tenney (Grand Rapids, Mich.: Zondervan Publishing House, Regency Reference Library, 1975), vol. 5, p. 270.

From the issues Peter addressed, we observe another limitation: *religion is blinded to Christ's working.* The leaders could not deny the healing. The only explanation for this miracle was the mighty working of the resurrected Jesus. But their religious biases prevented them from seeing the truth.

As a result, they exhibited the third limitation Peter recognized:

> "And there is salvation in no one else; for there is no other name under heaven that has been given among men, by which we must be saved." (v. 12)

Although Peter clearly and succinctly preached salvation through Christ, *religion is unmoved by the gospel message.* Religion walks the path of love and good deeds, but eventually it faces a fork in the road: follow Christ or follow a religious system. This thought offends religious people because they believe salvation comes through their own goodness. They are unmoved by Christ's death for the sins of the world and are cold to their need for salvation.

Peter's message did not melt the Council members' hearts, but they were impressed with his boldness and eloquence.

> Now as they observed the confidence of Peter and John, and understood that they were uneducated and untrained men, they were marveling, and began to recognize them as having been with Jesus. And seeing the man who had been healed standing with them, they had nothing to say in reply. (vv. 13–14)

Peter's speech and the presence of the healed man must have caused some nervous shifting and sweaty foreheads in the Sanhedrin. They could argue theory, they could debate the law, but they couldn't refute the facts: ignorant men had spoken articulately, and a once-lame man could walk. So they said nothing. This illustrates the fourth limitation: *religion is silenced by transformed lives.*

The Decision: Exit Religion

The men on the Council glanced at each other, waiting for someone to respond. But when no one spoke, they dismissed Peter, John, and the healed man and discussed what to do next (v. 15).

The Issue

Behind closed doors, the Sanhedrin deliberated.

"What shall we do with these men? For the fact that a noteworthy miracle has taken place through them is apparent to all who live in Jerusalem, and we cannot deny it. But in order that it may not spread any further among the people, let us warn them to speak no more to any man in this name." (vv. 16–17)

They couldn't admit Peter was right—that would mean they had crucified the Son of God! Yet what about this irrefutable miracle? What about the great wave of public support for Peter and John? Caught between a rock and a hard place, they decided to do nothing except issue a warning.

The Warning

With all the remaining intimidation they could muster, the Council commanded Peter and John "not to speak or teach at all in the name of Jesus" (v. 18). But this was like standing in front of a freight train, holding up a hand, and saying, "Stop! I command it!" Christianity was gaining steam, and nothing or no one could stand in its way.

The Response

Peter and John's response to the Sanhedrin illustrated their determination to ride the message of Christ through to the end.

But Peter and John answered and said to them, "Whether it is right in the sight of God to give heed to you rather than to God, you be the judge; for we cannot stop speaking what we have seen and heard." (vv. 19–20)

Powerless to quiet them, the embarrassed Sanhedrin merely

threatened them further, [and] let them go (finding no basis on which they might punish them) on account of the people, because they were all glorifying God for what had happened; for the man was more than forty years old on whom this miracle of healing had been performed. (vv. 21–22)

And What about Me Today?

Reflecting on this encounter between religion and Christianity, we clearly see that the first thing we need in our lives is an authentic relationship with Jesus Christ. And the last thing we need is a substitute. Religion replaces following Jesus with following rules. If we place our faith in a religious system rather than in Christ, we may be moral churchgoers or respected citizens, but we won't know Christ's power . . . or His joy.

☀ *Living Insights* STUDY ONE

These days we have sugar substitutes, salt substitutes, and aspirin substitutes. We can make vegetable oil look like butter, vinyl look like leather, glass look like diamonds, and plastic look like wood. With all these imitations, it's hard to know what's authentic anymore.

The same can be said about Christianity. Does genuine Christianity mean wearing a Jesus T-shirt, humming the latest praise songs, attending sold-out seminars, or chairing the Sunday school social committee? These are all good, but they can be substitutes for the real thing.

What do you think authentic Christianity is? For some ideas, read 2 Corinthians 2:14–17 and 3:12–18.

One key word stands out in 2 Corinthians 3:18—Christianity is transformation—becoming more like Jesus. Religion substitutes this process with conformation—becoming more like the system.

Have you been substituting religious conformity for Christlike transformation? If so, in what ways?

How do you think you can change your focus from conformation to transformation?

_____

_____

_____

What would help you become a more authentic Christian—more like Jesus?

_____

_____

_____

🌅 Living Insights STUDY TWO

The same John who stood alongside Peter before the Sanhedrin wrote later, "He who has the Son has the life; he who does not have the Son of God does not have the life" (1 John 5:12). "That life," Ray Stedman elucidates, "is more than mere morality,"

> it is more than doctrinal accuracy, it is more than inoffensive gentility. . . . It is a far cry indeed from the mild compatibility that passes as Christianity in thousands of churches across the land. The Great Imitation is so widely accepted as genuine Christianity that the real thing is often regarded as a threat or a heresy whenever it appears.[4]

Is Christ's life within you a threat or a heresy to anyone you know? If so, has intimidation, tradition, or interrogation been used against you? In what ways?

_____

_____

_____

4. Ray C. Stedman, _Authentic Christianity_ (Portland, Oreg.: Multnomah Press, 1975), pp. 12–13.

If your Christianity has brought you pressure from friends or family members, consider their limitations as non-Christians:

- They lack the Spirit's filling.

- They are blind to Christ's working.

- They are often unmoved by the gospel message.

- They are silenced by transformed lives.

How can recognizing these limitations give you . . .

1. boldness in responding to your religious antagonists?

_____

_____

_____

2. compassion for them?

_____

_____

_____

3. a strategy for responding to them?

_____

_____

_____

Finally, look at Peter's words in Acts 4:8–12, 19–20. How do they help you know what to say to those who oppose you?

_____

_____

_____

Chapter 10

TOUGH WITHOUT, TENDER WITHIN

Acts 4:23–35

Wagons, ho!

A group of pioneer families head west to claim a piece of America for their own. To survive the journey, they bring with them everything they own, including a couple of extra rifles and a constitution tough enough to handle the rugged trail.

The early Christians had this same pioneer toughness. Imprisonments, persecutions, and martyrdom dotted the landscape before them. Yet in spite of the dangers, they pressed on. Resilient. Unbending. Determined.

These Christian pioneers were just as tough on the outside as they were tender on the inside. Moved by the needs of those around them, they sensed God's quiet call and carried His love to all who would listen.

Tough without, tender within.

We, on the other hand, are often the opposite: fragile without and stubborn within. God points us to a mountain to climb, a river to ford, or a bone-jarring trail to travel, but we refuse to budge from our easy chairs.

We can catch the spirit of those early believers through the principles found in today's lesson—principles that will pour a little courage into our canteens, strap some faith onto our backs, and prepare us to hit the trail. Wagons, ho!

Persecuted but Not Forsaken

What produced the pioneer qualities in the first Christians? We don't have to read far to see that suffering persecution was a key factor. Opposition taught those early disciples to stand strong in their beliefs while staying dependent on God and each other. Their initial taste of persecution came when Peter and John were imprisoned and interrogated by the Sanhedrin after Peter had healed a lame man (Acts 1.1–7).

Confronted by the top religious leaders of their day, the two apostles could have meekly backed down . . . but instead, they stood calm and confident, boldly repeating their message that Jesus was the only "name under heaven that has been given among men, by which we must be saved" (v. 12). That's toughness! Yet they had been tenderhearted enough to notice and heal the lame man, a beggar who had been cast out of society. Even the Council noticed their tender, Christlike hearts; as Luke tells us, they "began to recognize them as having been with Jesus" (v. 13b).

The Sanhedrin warned them not to preach about Christ anymore, but this threat did not shake the apostles' determination to spread the gospel. Jesus' love and power burned in their hearts and fired their resolve to talk about Him more, even if it meant persecution. But they were not alone in their determination. Not only did they have the Holy Spirit; they were able to draw strength from the body of Christ, for "the number of the men [who believed] came to be about five thousand" (v. 4b).

Threatened but Not Weakened

We might think that mature, confident believers like Peter and John didn't need to depend on anyone else. But the truth is, they needed a support system too.

A Report

> And when they had been released, they went to
> their own [companions],[1] and reported all that the
> chief priests and the elders had said to them. (v. 23)

Peter and John were probably still bruised physically from their imprisonment and emotionally from the verbal attacks of the religious leaders. They needed to be surrounded by people who cared for them, who would listen to them. They needed their Christian family.

To seek out and share our lives with other brothers and sisters in the Lord is no sign of weakness. In fact, sharing our hearts with others builds up our fortitude. Christian pioneers know the value of companionship on the trail.

---

1. The word *companions* was added by the editors to clarify the text. The original simply says, "they went to their own"—their own people, those with a kindred spirit who would accept them.

A Prayer

With ears tuned to every word of the apostles' experience, the people then "lifted up their voices to God with one accord" (v. 24a). Four characteristics about their prayer illustrate the people's tender hearts toward the Lord and their tough resolve to accomplish His will.

First, *the prayer began spontaneously.* The people broke out in prayer without anyone having to say, "Let us pray." It was impulsive and informal, like applause.

In our well-oiled, machinelike churches, we often confine our spirituality in little boxes of time: worship time, sermon time, prayer time. And in each box is a set of rules to follow. But the early believers had no boxes and no rules. They prayed and worshiped when the Spirit moved—no matter where, no matter when.

The second thing we observe is that *the prayer claimed God's sovereignty.* They called out to their Lord, acknowledging that He has made everything (v. 24b), He controls everything (vv. 25–27), and He has a purpose for everything (v. 28). Notice these three elements in their prayer:

> "O Lord, it is Thou who didst make the heaven and the earth and the sea, and all that is in them, who by the Holy Spirit, through the mouth of our father David Thy servant, didst say,
>> 'Why did the Gentiles rage,
>> And the peoples devise futile things?
>> The kings of the earth took their stand,
>> And the rulers were gathered together
>> Against the Lord, and against His Christ.'
> "For truly in this city there were gathered together against Thy holy servant Jesus, whom Thou didst anoint, both Herod and Pontius Pilate, along with the Gentiles and the peoples of Israel, to do whatever Thy hand and Thy purpose predestined to occur."
> (vv. 24b–28)

By recognizing that God had created the world and everyone in it, including their antagonists, they were turning all their concerns over to Him. Whether their enemies were the Gentiles, the kings of the earth, Herod, Pontius Pilate, or the Sanhedrin, God was in control. And everything would be accomplished according to His purpose.

"Lord, we don't know what your plan is," they were saying, "but we know that we're living under Your sovereign hand. You have predestined a direction in life for us that will build into us the things we need. Carry out Your plan and purpose. You don't even have to explain it to us."

What faith!

They were not finished, though. Next, we notice that *the prayer included two requests*.

"Lord," they asked, "take note of [our enemy's] threats" and "grant that Thy bond-servants may speak Thy word with all confidence" (v. 29). They didn't plead, "Lord, wipe out the Sanhedrin" or, "Lord, get us out of here!" They simply requested courage so they could speak His Word.

Finally, we see that *the prayer emphasized positive faith*. They did not have an entreaty for the Lord, only an anticipation: that He would heal and work signs and wonders through the name of Jesus (v. 30). Did God respond to their faith in Him?

An Answer

Because of their sensitivity toward the Lord and their rugged determination to follow His will, their prayer was answered in a mighty way.

> And when they had prayed, the place where they had gathered together was shaken, and they were all filled with the Holy Spirit, and began to speak the word of God with boldness. (v. 31)

More persecution awaited the young believers, but God reassured them, surrounding them with evidences of the Spirit's power and guidance. It was as if He were saying, "Keep on going. Leave the dangers and the details to Me. Just stay at your task of witnessing for My Son, and I'll give you the strength you need. Remember, I'm on your side!"

Attacked but Not Separated

The early church had climbed its first mountain of opposition. The believers' tough resolve had grown more rugged and their tender hearts more sensitive. And through this ordeal, the church grew together in unity.

Their Claim

Persecution has a tendency to draw people together, and these Christians claimed it had done just that.

> And the congregation of those who believed were of one heart and soul; and not one of them claimed that anything belonging to him was his own; but all things were common property to them. And with great power the apostles were giving witness to the resurrection of the Lord Jesus, and abundant grace was upon them all. (vv. 32–33)

But would they actually care for one another according to the abundant power and grace that had been given them?

Their Compassion

Verses 34 and 35 show that they did share their goods with each other, not by force but in love, as Christ taught.

> For there was not a needy person among them, for all who were owners of land or houses would sell them and bring the proceeds of the sales, and lay them at the apostles' feet; and they would be distributed to each, as any had need. (vv. 34–35)

Instructed but Not Involved

As we reflect on how these pioneer Christians responded to their difficult journey, four principles emerge that teach us how to become more pioneerlike . . . tough without, tender within.

First, we need *initiative*. Deep inside our lives, there must be a yearning to follow Christ. It starts with our desire, based on the fact that there is no safer, no more thrilling place than at His side, walking through life with Him.

Second, we need *compassion*. The early Christians saw a world that desperately needed to know about Christ. Do you see that same world? Are you filled with compassion to help others find Him?

Third, we need *vulnerability*. Being tender in spirit means opening up to a family of believers, just like the apostles did when they were released from prison. It means taking a risk, being willing to reach out to others in love—which brings us to our fourth principle.

We need *love*. C. S. Lewis wrote:

To love at all is to be vulnerable. Love anything, and your heart will certainly be wrung and possibly be broken. If you want to make sure of keeping it intact, you must give your heart to no one, not even to an animal. Wrap it carefully round with hobbies and little luxuries; avoid all entanglements; lock it up safe in the casket or coffin of your selfishness. But in that casket—safe, dark, motionless, airless—it will change. It will not be broken; it will become unbreakable, impenetrable, irredeemable. . . . The only place outside Heaven where you can be per-fectly safe from all the dangers and perturbations of love is Hell.[2]

Let the early Christians inspire you to a more genuine faith—a faith that is tough enough to handle the ruggedness of following Christ, and tender enough to risk loving others.

☀ Living Insights

Peter learned a lot about persecution from his experiences in these early days of the church. He later wrote in his epistle,

> Beloved, do not be surprised at the fiery ordeal
> among you, which comes upon you for your testing,
> as though some strange thing were happening to you.
> (1 Pet. 4:12)

Even Jesus said: "If they persecuted Me, they will also persecute you" (John 15:20b). So don't be surprised when unbelievers throw stones, say hateful words, or spread nasty rumors because of your Christianity. In fact, be more surprised if they don't.

Have you born the brunt of a sarcastic comment, a cold shoulder, a passed-over promotion, or some other persecution because of your beliefs? Describe the situation here.

_____

_____

2. C. S. Lewis, *The Four Loves* (San Diego, Calif.: Harcourt Brace Jovanovich, Publishers, 1960), p. 169.

As a result of this mistreatment, have you felt like retaliating? What guidance can you glean from the prayer at the beginning of this lesson that will help you avoid feelings of revenge? Read again Acts 4:24–30, especially verse 29.

_____

_____

_____

The early believers prayed for courage to talk about Christ in spite of persecution. They expressed their faith in God, who is sovereign over the universe as well as their lives. Write out your own prayer of faith in the Lord, following this pattern:

1. Claim God's sovereignty by recognizing that He is Lord over the universe, He is in control of your situation, and He has a predestined purpose for you.

_____

_____

_____

_____

2. Ask the Lord to take note of your persecution and to give you courage to speak His Word.

_____

_____

_____

_____

3. Express positive faith by anticipating the marvelous things God is going to do through your witness.

_____

_____

_____

_____

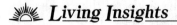

Christians should be adventurers at heart. God has given us the world to step into as His messengers of hope, and we just need to open our eyes to the possibilities that await us. The book *How to Be a World-Class Christian* includes numerous ways we can be world-aware Christians. The author, Paul Borthwick, calls it "going global." For starters:

- Host a missionary and let your family hear about life in a foreign culture.

- Write to missionaries.

- House an exchange student.

- Keep a stack of prayer cards at the dinner table and pray for one missionary every time there is a family meal.

- As a family support an international project or a child overseas.

For an even greater adventure, Borthwick suggests learning a new language, volunteering for a homeless shelter, heading up an ethnic children's group, or offering your skills to an inner-city ministry.

And for the greatest adventure of all, go on a cross-cultural, short-term missions project. Extend an overseas business trip to visit and encourage national Christians. Or plan some "vacations with a purpose" to help mission organizations with a building or evangelism project.[3]

The world awaits!

---

3. See Paul Borthwick, *How to Be a World-Class Christian* (Wheaton, Ill.: Victor Books, Scripture Press Publications, 1991), pp. 122–29. For information on short-term mission projects, see the section "Books for Probing Further" at the end of this study guide.

Chapter 11

A DEADLY GAME

Acts 4:36–5:11

Let's play pretend," says the pigtailed girl to her little sister. "I'll be the actress, and you can be the audience."

"Why do I always have to be the . . . aw–biance?"

"Because, daaling, I'm a staar," drawls the older one, taking on airs. "Now, ask me for my autograph."

Children love pretending. But they aren't the only ones who play pretend games. Adults play them as well. How often have we laughed gaily to appear fun-loving? Or posed a deep question to appear intellectual? Or given money to appear generous? Or exposed another's sins to appear holy? All can be games of pretend, and one word describes us when we play them—hypocrites.

Originating in Greek theater, the word *hypocrite* initially referred to an actor, who donned elaborate masks to play his roles.[1] When Christians put on masks, they play roles too. What does God think of our playacting? He takes it seriously—a fact Ananias and Sapphira discovered when their pretend game turned deadly.

Authentic Generosity

Like thousands of others at that time, Ananias and his wife Sapphira were riding the spiritual tide that was surging through Jerusalem. The Holy Spirit had come as Jesus promised, the believers were boldly proclaiming the gospel, and the church was enjoying heavenly fellowship—*koinōnia*.

In Acts 4:32–35, Luke describes these glory days in general terms, stating that "those who believed were of one heart and soul" and that

> not one of them claimed that anything belonging to him was his own; but all things were common property to them. (v. 32b)

---

1. G. Abbott-Smith defines the Greek term *hupokritēs* literally as "a stage player, actor" and metaphorically as "a pretender, dissembler, hypocrite." See *A Manual Greek Lexicon of the New Testament*, 3d ed. (Edinburgh, Scotland: T. & T. Clark, 1977), p. 461.

Those who owned property were even selling their investments in order to help needy believers (vv. 34–35). Modeling this selfless spirit was Barnabas.[2] According to verses 36–37, he sold a tract of land and offered the money to the apostles, who would distribute the funds to the poorer members of the church. Undoubtedly, the news of Barnabas' generosity encouraged the entire assembly.

Pretentious Hypocrisy

Then, abruptly, the wind shifts. The selflessness of Barnabas described in chapter 4 gives way to the selfishness of Ananias and Sapphira portrayed in chapter 5.

> But a certain man named Ananias, with his wife Sapphira, sold a piece of property, and kept back some of the price for himself, with his wife's full knowledge, and bringing a portion of it, he laid it at the apostles' feet. (Acts 5:1–2)

We are not told why this couple wanted to sell their property. But we can guess that they envied the approval the church must have given Barnabas. Maybe they thought, "We, too, would like to hear some applause."

If this was true, then their motives were impure. But what about their actions? Was it wrong for them to sell the land and give only a portion of the proceeds to the church? No, not necessarily. They sinned when they *pretended* to give it all.

The nature of their hypocrisy will become clear to us when we uncover the specifics of the situation. As we do, we'll notice a definite four-step cycle of events.

Cycle of Events

Let's see how Ananias and Sapphira progress through this cycle, starting with the one who delivers the gift to the apostles, the husband.

Declaration of Ananias. Although Luke leaves out Ananias' words, we observe him bringing the money from the sale of the property, minus a portion, and laying it at the apostles' feet (v. 2). Perhaps he says, "We sold our land, and here is all the money." Or

---

2. His name was Joseph, but the apostles called him Barnabas, which means "Son of Encouragement" (v. 36).

perhaps he implies by his actions that he is donating the full price. In either case, he is lying.

Pretension before the body. When Ananias dons the mask of a selfless giver, he exhibits a false front to the church. How much better for him to have been honest about keeping back some of the money—as we'll see as our story progresses.

Confrontation by Peter. After Ananias lays down his offering, Peter confronts him:

> "Ananias, why has Satan filled your heart to lie to the Holy Spirit, and to keep back some of the price of the land? While it remained unsold, did it not remain your own? And after it was sold, was it not under your control? Why is it that you have conceived this deed in your heart? You have not lied to men, but to God." (vv. 3–4)

Through divine discernment, Peter perceives that Ananias is lying. He points out the sin with penetrating accuracy. Like Nathan, who rebuked the adulterous David (2 Sam. 12:1–15); and like Elisha, who interrogated his greedy servant Gehazi (2 Kings 5:1 –27); Peter calls down Ananias with prophetic passion. Surely it would have been easier for Peter to overlook this one little lie, but for the spiritual health of the church, it is necessary to bring it to light.

Judgment from God. God's judgment swiftly follows Peter's confrontation.

> And as he heard these words, Ananias fell down and breathed his last; and great fear came upon all who heard of it. And the young men arose and covered him up, and after carrying him out, they buried him. (Acts 5:5–6)

Death strikes Ananias immediately. Those who see him fall gasp in fear and, for an unearthly moment, stand motionless . . . staring. Finally, some men wrap up the body and bury it. Ananias is gone.

> Now there elapsed an interval of about three hours. (v. 7a)

Sapphira begins to wonder why her husband is taking so long to deliver the money to the apostles. She had been in on the conspiracy, but no one would know. What would be the harm, anyway? *Why is Ananias taking so long?*

She decides to go to where the apostles are gathered. When she enters the room, Peter speaks to her.

> "Tell me whether you sold the land for such and such a price?" (v. 8a)

He gives her a chance to confess her sin. "Was the money given by Ananias the full amount of the sale?" Feigning innocence, Sapphira replies,

> "Yes, that was the price." (v. 8b)

As she declares this lie, the cycle of events repeats. She makes her pretense before the body, and Peter confronts her:

> "Why is it that you have agreed together to put the Spirit of the Lord to the test? Behold, the feet of those who have buried your husband are at the door, and they shall carry you out as well." (v. 9)

Then the Lord judges her as He had her husband.

> And she fell immediately at his feet, and breathed her last; and the young men came in and found her dead, and they carried her out and buried her beside her husband. And great fear came upon the whole church, and upon all who heard of these things. (vv. 10–11)

The harshness of God's judgment on Ananias and Sapphira takes our breath away. What was so hideous about their sin?

Analysis of Sin

In the first place, their deed was premeditated. It was not an innocent mistake or oversight. They had planned to deceive the apostles from the start.

In addition, at the heart of their action was pride. Their real desire wasn't to make a donation to their church; they desired to grab some glory for themselves. And once they were found out, they were unwilling to be humble and admit the truth.

Serious Responsibility

Through God's sudden judgment of Ananias and Sapphira, He

taught the early church a never-to-be-forgotten lesson about the seriousness of hypocrisy. As a result, the church's reputation remained intact and its witness for Christ continued with integrity.

Today, one of the most common complaints about Christians is that we are hypocrites. To avoid that label, we need to take seriously our responsibility to be honest with ourselves, with God, and with the body.

Responsibility to Ourselves

Integrity begins when we examine our motives. Are we facing the truth, being honest about *why* we serve or teach or give? Are our motives pure, or are we acting out of pride, in order to gain favor from others? We each need to plead, like the psalmist,

> Search me, O God, and know my heart;
> Try me and know my anxious thoughts;
> And see if there be any hurtful way in me,
> And lead me in the everlasting way.
> (Ps. 139:23–24)

Responsibility to God

When Ananias and Sapphira carried out their plan of deception, they lied to the Holy Spirit, not just to the church. That lie, far from gaining them the glory they sought, cost them everything. Hiding behind useless masks will bring us only misery, as David discovered when he tried to hide his sin from God.

> How blessed is the man to whom the Lord does
>   not impute iniquity,
> And in whose spirit there is no deceit!
> When I kept silent about my sin, my body wasted
>   away
> Through my groaning all day long.
> (Ps. 32:2–3)

We are responsible to God for our actions, and try as we might, it's impossible to hide them from Him.

Responsibility to the Body

Finally, we are responsible to other believers—those people we need the most. They always suffer when the truth exposes our hypocrisy. That is why Paul wrote:

Let love be without hypocrisy. Abhor what is
evil; cling to what is good. (Rom. 12:9)

It's often easy to pretend we love others, to say words we don't
mean and make promises we can't keep. It is much more difficult
to drop our masks and forsake our securities to truly love others.
But it is in authentic loving that the body of Christ unites, and it
is in integrity that the world sees Jesus in us.

 ## Living Insights

George MacDonald defined hypocrisy as

> the desire to look better than you are; the hiding of
> things you do, because you would not be supposed
> to do them, because you would be ashamed to have
> them known where you are known. The doing of
> them is foul; the hiding of them, in order to appear
> better than you are, is fouler still.[3]

Ananias and Sapphira desired to look better than they were.
They hid their actions for fear of shame. As a result, their offering
to the Lord was "fouler still."

Recall your most recent religious involvement, whether a home
Bible study, a service project, or a Sunday morning worship service.
Review the event in your mind, from leaving your house to coming
home afterward.

Did you have any desire to appear better than you were? If so,
describe this motivation and how it manifested itself in your actions.

_____

_____

_____

Did you attempt to hide something through these actions? What
were you hiding?

_____

3. As quoted in *George MacDonald: Selections from His Greatest Works*, ed. David L. Neuhouser
(Wheaton, Ill.: Scripture Press Publications, Victor Books, 1990), p. 59.

If there is hidden sin in your life, stop pretending you are holier than you really are. Find a small group of Christians with whom you can be real, with whom you can remove your mask, with whom you can experience Christ's cleansing forgiveness. Don't let secrets turn you into a hypocrite.

C. H. Spurgeon penned this warning:

> Coals of fire cannot be concealed beneath the most sumptuous apparel, they will betray themselves with smoke and flame. Neither can pet sins be long hidden beneath the most ostentatious profession of faith; they will sooner or later discover themselves, and burn sad holes in a person's reputation. *Sin needs quenching in the Savior's blood, not concealing under the garb of religion.* (emphasis added)[4]

🌄 Living Insights

Do you have a small group to which you are accountable? If not, Lyman Coleman and Marty Scales suggest that you can start one by finding one person who shares your desire.

Who can you ask to be your partner in launching a small group?

Set a time to meet with this person. When you meet, decide on several others you can ask to participate. Keep the group small at first. Then plan your first meeting.

At the first meeting, challenge the group to commit themselves to a covenant that includes the purpose and goals of the group; when, where, and how often you will meet; and certain group disciplines: consistent attendance, equal participation, strict confidentiality, mutual accountability, unlimited accessibility, and a willingness to reach out to others.

4. Charles Spurgeon, *The Quotable Spurgeon* (Wheaton, Ill.: Harold Shaw Publishers, 1990), p. 349.

Organize your meetings to allow time for three basic ingredients: Bible study, group support, and outreach. Finally, establish a closure date for the group—a date when the group will either disband or recovenant for another period.[5]

Commit yourself to a small group soon. Through accountability you can close the door on hypocrisy and open up authenticity in your life.

In addition to Coleman and Scales' book on small groups, footnoted below, we recommend the following works:

Griffin, Em. *Getting Together.* Downers Grove, Ill.: InterVarsity Press, 1982.

McBride, Neal. F. *How to Lead Small Groups.* Colorado Springs, Colo.: NavPress, 1990.

Williams, Dan. *Seven Myths about Small Groups.* Downers Grove, Ill.: InverVarsity Press, 1991.

5. See Lyman Coleman and Marty Scales, *Serendipity Training Manual for Groups* (Littleton, Colo.: Serendipity House, 1989), pp. 3–7.

Chapter 12

WE OVERWHELMINGLY CONQUER

Acts 5:12–42

Who shall separate us from the love of Christ?
> Shall tribulation,
>> or distress,
>>> or persecution,
>>>> or famine,
>>>>> or nakedness,
>>>>>> or peril,
>>>>>>> or sword?

Just as it is written,
> "For Thy sake we are being put to death all day
> long;
> We were considered as sheep to be slaughtered."

But in all these things we overwhelmingly conquer through Him who loved us. (Rom. 8:35–37, emphasis added)

Contained within these stirring lines is the central message of our lesson. Like sheep led to slaughter, the apostles were persecuted, imprisoned, and beaten for teaching the gospel. But through Christ, the Great Shepherd, they overwhelmingly conquered.

As we follow their footprints through Acts 5:12–42, we'll see for ourselves God's victorious power in their lives. Our story begins at Solomon's portico, where we find the apostles at the hub of much excitement.

Power on the Porch

Solomon's portico was a roofed colonnade that resembled a long porch, stretching along the eastern side of the temple courtyard.[1] Here the believers had gathered, and "at the hands of the apostles

---

1. J. B. Payne, *The Zondervan Pictorial Encyclopedia of the Bible,* ed. Merrill C. Tenney (Grand Rapids, Mich.: Zondervan Publishing House, Regency Reference Library, 1976), vol. 5, p. 479.

many signs and wonders were taking place among the people"
(v. 12a). As a result,

> all the more believers in the Lord, multitudes of men
> and women, were constantly added to their number;
> to such an extent that they even carried the sick out
> into the streets, and laid them on cots and pallets,
> so that when Peter came by, at least his shadow
> might fall on any one of them. (vv. 14–16)

These miracles underscored the Spirit's dynamic presence in the
apostles' lives.[2] They may have been ordinary men, but the Holy
Spirit enabled them to be the voice and hands of Jesus, drawing
hundreds more to Himself.

Joy in the Jail

> But the high priest rose up, along with all his asso-
> ciates (that is the sect of the Sadducees), and they
> were filled with jealousy; and they laid hands on the
> apostles, and put them in a public jail. (vv. 17–18)

Tentacles of jealousy gripped the hearts of the religious leaders
when they saw the people eagerly embrace this new teaching. Enraged, they ordered the apostles locked up, hoping to quell the
threatening movement.

> But an angel of the Lord during the night opened
> the gates of the prison, and taking them out he said,
> "Go your way, stand and speak to the people in the
> temple the whole message of this Life." (vv. 19–20)

Lloyd John Ogilvie comments on the angel's commands:

> Here were marching orders to go offer the grandest
> gift the Lord had to give for the greatest need the
> people had. Go take your stand. Tell people about
> Life.[3]

God issues these same directives to us. He doesn't want us to

---

2. Our word *dynamic* is a derivation of the Greek word for power, the power that Jesus had
promised them: "But you shall receive power"—*dunamis*—"when the Holy Spirit has come
upon you" (Acts 1:8).

3. Lloyd John Ogilvie, *Drumbeat of Love* (Waco, Tex.: Word Books, 1976), p. 76.

conceal our new life; instead, He empowers us to speak about the gospel whenever and wherever possible.

Teaching in the Temple

The apostles returned to the temple and began teaching with renewed fervor (v. 21a). How their words must have rung with authority! They had just experienced Christ's power firsthand. Now they joyfully shouted Christ's message to all who will hear.

Meanwhile . . .

> When the high priest and his associates had come, they called the Council together, even all the Senate of the sons of Israel, and sent orders to the prison house for them to be brought. But the officers who came did not find them in the prison; and they returned, and reported back, saying, "We found the prison house locked quite securely and the guards standing at the doors; but when we had opened up, we found no one inside." Now when the captain of the temple guard and the chief priests heard these words, they were greatly perplexed about them as to what would come of this. (vv. 21b–24)

Just then a messenger arrived with some embarrassing news.

> "Behold, the men whom you put in prison are standing in the temple and teaching the people!" (v. 25b)

"What . . . how can this be?" These men hadn't yet learned that when God works, He often defies explanation. He moves wherever He wishes and does whatever He pleases. Not even prison bars can block His power when He invades the lives of people willing to take a stand for Him.

Courage before the Court

Quickly and quietly, to avoid a scene, the captain of the temple guard and his officers retrieved the apostles and brought them before the Council (vv. 26–27a). Motivated by fear, the high priest lashed out with his indictment:

> We gave you strict orders not to continue teaching in this name, and behold, you have filled Jerusalem

with your teaching, and intend to bring this man's blood upon us." (v. 28)

Calmly and courageously the apostles responded:

> "We must obey God rather than men. The God of our fathers raised up Jesus, whom you had put to death by hanging Him on a cross. He is the one whom God exalted to His right hand as a Prince and a Savior, to grant repentance to Israel, and forgiveness of sins. And we are witnesses of these things; and so is the Holy Spirit, whom God has given to those who obey Him." (vv. 29b–32)

Their determination to obey God liberated them from fear and released the Spirit's power in their lives. As Ogilvie observes:

> We cannot expect the joy and energy of his infilling if we are saying "No!" to what we know from our prayers we should do.
>
> Obedience is like a thermostat. It opens the flow of the Spirit for the needs around us. The cold of the world calls for the heat and warmth of the fire of the Holy Spirit within us.[4]

The apostles' courage insulted the proud officials, who "were cut to the quick and were intending to slay them" (v. 33b). If not for the Lord's intervention, the apostles would have been killed then and there. How did the Lord step in?

He used unbelieving Gamaliel, a respected Pharisee, to defuse the explosive situation. Gamaliel sent the apostles out of the chamber and spoke frankly to the Council members:

> "Men of Israel, take care what you propose to do with these men. For some time ago Theudas rose up, claiming to be somebody; and a group of about four hundred men joined up with him. And he was slain; and all who followed him were dispersed and came to nothing. After this man Judas of Galilee rose up in the days of the census, and drew away some people after him, he too perished, and all those who followed him were scattered. And so in the present

4. Ogilvie, *Drumbeat of Love,* p. 82.

case, I say to you, stay away from these men and let them alone, for if this plan or action should be of men, it will be overthrown; but if it is of God, you will not be able to overthrow them; or else you may even be found fighting against God." (vv. 35–39)

Reluctantly persuaded, the Council summoned the apostles. Instead of executing them, they beat them and sent them away with another warning not to speak of Jesus (v. 40)—a warning the apostles would again disobey.

Sharing in the Streets

Each lash of the whip only strengthened the apostles' resolve to witness for Christ. They may have come before the Sanhedrin as defenseless sheep before the slaughter, but with the Spirit's power, they left as conquerors.

They went on their way from the presence of the Council, rejoicing that they had been considered worthy to suffer shame for His name. And every day, in the temple and from house to house, they kept right on teaching and preaching Jesus as the Christ. (vv. 41–42)

Conquering Then and Now

Most of us will never experience the degree of suffering endured by the first-century believers. But perhaps as a Christian you've been the target of ridicule or reproach. You, too, can overwhelmingly conquer when you remember two principles.

First, *opposition may mean you're in God's will, not out of it.* The apostles weren't out of God's will because they experienced hardship. On the contrary, trouble struck because they were obeying His will. If people persecute you because you are following God, don't give up. Keep obeying, and God will transform your trial into triumph.

Second, *determination will mean you'll have to stand against man's opinion, rather than with it.* By determining to follow God's will, your course will collide with what the world says you should do. Some will advise you to "take the easy way." Others may complain, "Quit that—you're making us look bad!" When you hear those remarks,

let the apostles' words guide your path: "We must obey God rather than men" (v. 29).

☀ _Living Insights_ STUDY ONE

"We must obey God rather than men." This familiar statement tends to slip quickly off our tongues without serious consideration. Let's take the time now to ponder its implications.

Are people pointing you in one direction while God's Word tells you to go another? Complete the following sentences that apply to you:

My spouse tells me to _____.

But God's Word tells me to _____.

My parents tell me to _____.

But God's Word tells me to _____.

My friends tell me to _____.

But God's Word tells me to _____.

My boss tells me to _____.

But God's Word tells me to _____.

My coworkers tell me to _____.

But God's Word tells me to _____.

Although the Bible doesn't clearly point the way we should go every time, pathways involving cheating, stealing, and lying, for instance, are always dead-end roads. At these times, we must obey God rather than friends, family, or even bosses. Will you commit right now to follow God's way no matter what the cost? No matter who wants you to go their way?

The apostles suffered because they were loyal to Christ. How did they respond? With joy!

Why?

They rejoiced because "they had been considered worthy to suffer shame for His name" (Acts 5:41b). They felt honored to experience the same ridicule Christ endured—the same threats, the same sting of the whip. They were glad to be able, as Peter later wrote, to "share the sufferings of Christ" (1 Pet. 4:13).

Read Peter's words in 1 Peter 4:12–14. What other reasons do you see for rejoicing while suffering? Note especially verses 13b and 14b.

Peter warns us, however, that not all suffering is honorable. What distinguishes suffering that produces glory from suffering that produces shame (vv. 15–16)?

If we do suffer for following Christ, what should be our overall response (v. 19)?

There is no joy in suffering for doing wrong. Neither is there joy for suffering as a result of our foolishness. Purposely inciting ridicule or retaliation from unbelievers is not suffering shame for Christ's name. John White further distinguishes suffering as a Christian from other forms of suffering:

> Christian suffering has to do with the cross I take up and heave on my back. It is suffering because of a deliberate choice. The kind of cross to which Christ refers is not a "cross" of rheumatism or of the petty annoyances . . . in life. It is the badge of a

99

true follower of Jesus. It may take any form—sickness, hunger, loneliness, persecution, death.[5]

Are you willing to take up Jesus' cross? To obey Christ even in suffering? In alienation? Embarrassment? Loss?

If you are, you will find it the only way to true joy, to ecstatic fellowship with Jesus.

———◆———

O Jesus, I have promised
    To serve thee to the end:
Be thou for ever near me,
    My Master and my Friend!
I shall not fear the battle,
    If thou art by my side,
Nor wander from the pathway,
    If thou wilt be my Guide. . . .

O let me see thy footmarks,
    And in them plant my own!
My hope to follow duly
    Is in thy strength alone.
O guide me, call me, draw me,
    Uphold me to the end!
At last in heaven receive me,
    My Saviour and my Friend![6]

5. John White, *Magnificent Obsession*, rev. ed. (Downers Grove, Ill.: InterVarsity Press, 1990), p. 75.

6. John E. Bode in *The Best Loved Hymns and Prayers of the American People*, ed. Harold Vincent Milligan (Garden City, N.Y.: Garden City Publishing Co., Halcyon House, 1942), pp. 120–21.

Chapter 13

OPERATION ICEBERG
Acts 6:1–7

Some churches are a lot like icebergs.

Like icebergs?

Sure. For one thing, icebergs are enormous. This certainly describes the first-century Jerusalem church. At last count, in Acts 4:4, the membership had swelled to about five thousand, numbering only the men.

For another thing, icebergs just float along with the current. The early church, too, was in danger of floating aimlessly, allowing growth to knock it off course.

Yet another characteristic of icebergs is that they carry a lot of debris along with them. In Acts 6, we see disturbing signs that this young congregation had already collected the debris of jealousy, suspicion, and prejudice. If that debris wasn't disposed of soon the church could crack and break apart. A strategy was necessary—a strategy we'll call Operation Iceberg.

Perils of Rapid Growth

Operation Iceberg addressed the perils of rapid growth we see in some of today's churches. Let's look at a few of these perils before we examine the solution the Jerusalem church enacted.

First, constant busyness, daily decisions, and ever-pressing needs tend to cause the congregation to have an *uncertainty of purpose*. In the beginning, the ministry's grand design may have been clear, but as the church grows, fewer people can recall the reason for all their activity.

Another peril is *fuzzy priorities*. A wider ministry sparks additional demands. As a result, church leaders may begin throwing aside yesterday's priorities to put out today's fires. Soon, what should be most important places second to what is most urgent.

Also, along with rapid growth comes a *tendency toward professionalism*. Escalating ministries sometimes hire a staff of pros to take over the work. The result: a church full of spectators. Instead, the church staff should equip the membership to minister by cultivating their spiritual gifts.

The final peril is a *loss of individual significance*. It's easy to get lost in the crowd, to think no one cares about your problems. Just the size of the congregation is intimidating. Who wants to make waves by asking a question or stating a need?

As we shall see, it's this fourth peril that particularly endangered the early church. To meet some members' needs, the leaders had to change their organization.

Structure of Early Church

As we skim Acts 6:1–7, we can pick out three groups of people that made up the church's organizational structure. The following chart identifies and defines them.

Title	Role
Disciples/Congregation	Body of believers in Jerusalem
The Twelve/Apostles	Divinely appointed overseers (also called elders or pastors)
Seven Men (Deacons)	Assistants to elders in delegated areas

We are familiar with the "disciples" (vv. 1–2, 5, 7) and with the "twelve" (vv. 2, 6). But who were the "seven men" (v. 3), and what were their responsibilities?

The appointment of seven men was a response to a problem that threatened to break apart the early church. This wise strategy employed by the apostles was the central component of Operation Iceberg.

Example of Wise Leadership

We do not have to read far into verse 1 before we encounter the problem. The apostles heard of it when a group of believers voiced a complaint.

Explanation of Complaint

> Now at this time while the disciples were increasing in number, a complaint arose on the part of the Hellenistic Jews against the native Hebrews, because their widows were being overlooked in the

daily serving of food. (v. 1)

Neglecting the Hellenistic widows reflected a loss of individual significance in the rapidly growing Jerusalem church. With a few pertinent cultural facts, William Barclay helps us to better understand this problem.

> In the synagogue there was a routine custom. Two collectors went round the market and the private houses every Friday morning and made a collection for the needy partly in money and partly in goods. Later in the day this was distributed. . . . In addition to this a house-to-house collection was made daily for those in pressing need.
>
> It is clear that the Christian Church had taken over this custom. But amidst the Jews themselves there was a cleavage. In the Christian Church there were two kinds of Jews. There were the Jerusalem and the Palestinian Jews who spoke Aramaic. . . . There were also Jews from foreign countries who had come up for Pentecost and made the great discovery of Christ. Many of these had been away from Palestine for generations; they had forgotten their Hebrew and spoke only Greek. The natural consequence was that the spiritually snobbish Aramaic-speaking Jews looked down on the foreign Jews. This contempt affected the daily distribution of alms.[1]

Whether or not overlooking the non-Hebrew widows was intentional, cultural prejudices fueled the turbulent feelings among the Hellenistic Christians. "Unfair! Favoritism!" they cried, and cracks zigzagged across the base of the church.

What would the apostles do?

Their natural response might have been to distribute the food themselves. But they took a different approach, one that revealed their wise leadership.

Declaration of Priorities

The apostles' first step was to state their priorities.

---

1. William Barclay, *The Acts of the Apostles*, rev. ed., The Daily Study Bible Series (Philadelphia, Pa.: Westminster Press, 1976), pp. 51–52.

And the twelve summoned the congregation of the disciples and said, "It is not desirable for us to neglect the word of God in order to serve tables. . . . We will devote ourselves to prayer, and to the ministry of the word." (vv. 2, 4)

The Greek word for *desirable* means "fit" or "pleasing."[2] It was not pleasing to the Lord for the apostles to distribute the food. Their priorities were prayer and preaching the Word of God. Becoming too involved in personally meeting the needs of these widows would cause them to compromise their calling.

For any growing ministry to have continued impact, the leaders must be devoted to these same two priorities. Too often, leaders become entrenched in trying to meet the overwhelming flood of physical and emotional needs in the church. When this happens, spiritual moorings snap, and the ministry drifts along with any prevailing current.

Even so, needs must still be met. But how?

Correction of Difficulty

As the apostles looked out on the vast congregation, they announced their plan:

"Select from among you, brethren, seven men of good reputation, full of the Spirit and of wisdom, whom we may put in charge of this task." (v. 3)

The apostles delegated the responsibility to others so they could continue their own duties. Notice three components of their delegation. First, the seven men were to be *selected.* The apostles used a Greek word here that means to "inspect" or "examine." They did not want just the first seven volunteers; instead they instructed the congregation to thoughtfully evaluate the men of the assembly and then choose seven. Second, they were to be *qualified*—reputable, Spirit-filled, and wise. Last, they were to *take leadership*, to supervise the work skillfully.

Selection of Helpers

And the statement found approval with the whole

---

2. Fritz Rienecker, A *Linguistic Key to the Greek New Testament* (Grand Rapids, Mich.: Zondervan Publishing House, Regency Reference Library, 1976), p. 274.

congregation; and they chose Stephen, a man full of faith and of the Holy Spirit, and Philip, Prochorus, Nicanor, Timon, Parmenas and Nicolas, a proselyte from Antioch. And these they brought before the apostles; and after praying, they laid their hands on them. (vv. 5–6)

Exhibiting remarkable unity, the congregation applauded the plan and chose the men.[3] The selection process itself is a mystery to us, but two results are certain: the apostles' twofold ministry of prayer and the Word continued unhindered, and the problem of favoritism was solved.

Reaction of People

The apostles' expert leadership mended the cracks that had begun to form in the church . . . an iceberg on the brink of disintegrating was restored and grew even larger.

> And the word of God kept on spreading; and the number of the disciples continued to increase greatly in Jerusalem, and a great many of the priests were becoming obedient to the faith. (v. 7)

Principles of Timeless Value

What could have happened if the apostles hadn't judiciously guided the church through this perilous corridor? The Greek Christians could have split off from the Hebrews; the movement could have been weakened; the spreading flame could have been extinguished. But through God's grace, the opposite occurred—the flame burned even brighter.

From this experience, we can learn valuable lessons that will help us when we confront problems in our own churches.

Strong leadership doesn't guarantee an absence of problems. Even with the twelve highly gifted apostles in the lead, the church still endured difficulties. In our churches as well, we should not be surprised when frictions and factions cause problems.

Rapid growth doesn't excuse unmet needs. Busy leaders may be tempted to dismiss certain complaints as superfluous, but with wis-

---

3. Interestingly, all seven men had Greek names, which probably ensured a fair distribution of food to the Hellenistic widows.

dom they can strategize a solution to meet the needs without losing sight of their priorities.

Concerned involvement doesn't require losing priorities. Through delegation, pastors and leaders don't have to be overwhelmed by the hundreds of needs that come their way. They can guard their time for prayer and for the ministry of the Word.

A large church doesn't mean an ineffective ministry. Through strategic planning, even large ministries can have a personal touch so that the Word of God can keep on spreading.

Essentials of Every Church

As your church grows, the following essentials will keep it on course and protect it from the perils of expansion.[4]

Understanding the purpose of your church is the first essential. God established the church to equip Christians to minister to others (see Eph. 4:11–12). We accomplish this through four objectives that form the acronym *WIFE:* Worship, Instruction, Fellowship, and Expression.[5]

The way we carry out these objectives is the second essential and involves our style of ministry. The following style characteristics describe a growing church:

- teaching that is biblical, not philosophical,

- activities that emphasize spiritual gifts, not religious programs,

- an attitude that is open and balanced, not exclusive and extreme.

Founded on these essentials, the early church spiritually transformed their city. These principles are still operating today and can vitalize your church with the same irresistible appeal.

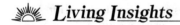 *Living Insights*

First, through hypocrisy, Ananias and Sapphira attempted to corrupt the church from within (Acts 5:1–11). Then, through

---

4. For an elaboration of these essentials of ministry, see chapters 2–5 of the book *Rise and Shine* by Charles R. Swindoll (Portland, Oreg.: Multnomah Press, 1989).

5. Expression involves missions, evangelism, and discipleship—the expressions of our faith.

persecution, the Jewish leaders tried to crush the church from without (vv. 12–42). But as we saw in this chapter,

> the devil's next attack was the cleverest of the three. Having failed to overcome the church by either persecution or corruption, he now tried distraction. If he could preoccupy the apostles with social administration, which though essential was not their calling, they would neglect their God-given responsibilities to pray and to preach, and so leave the church without any defence against false doctrine.[6]

Has Satan used this technique of distraction to cause you to neglect your Christian priorities? Think about this question as it applies to the four objectives of the church. How does Satan distract you . . .

- From worshiping the Lord?

_____

_____

- From learning God's Word?

_____

_____

- From genuine fellowship?

_____

_____

- From expressing your faith to others?

_____

_____

Dressed in a tattered widow's gown, the apostles' distraction was

6. John Stott, *The Spirit, the Church, and the World* (Downers Grove, Ill.: InterVarsity Press, 1990), p. 120.

particularly deceptive. What kind of cold-hearted person could turn down a defenseless widow's cry for help? But if the apostles had become personally involved, they would have neglected their pastoral priorities; for them, the worthy cause of helping the widows was a distraction. It was sin.

How can you know if a good cause is an opportunity or a distraction? First, know your priorities. Then rely on the Spirit for discernment. Finally, remember that it is all right to say no to a good thing in order to say yes to God's best.

☀ *Living Insights* STUDY TWO

What if the apostles had responded like we often do?

Peter: "Well, if we wake up earlier and go to bed later . . ."
John: "If we skip lunch and work Saturdays . . ."
Andrew: "If we cut out family time—they'll understand—and keep a more efficient schedule . . ."
James: "Then we can handle this widow problem and everything else we have to do."

Fortunately, they knew their limits. They couldn't pray and minister the Word and handle a hundred other concerns of the church . . . and keep their sanity!

Do you know your limits? How can you tell when you've exceeded them?

_____

_____

_____

Do you need to reevaluate your involvements in order to have time for what is really important? If so, what needs changing?

_____

_____

_____

Chapter 14
A WISE MAN UNDER PRESSURE
Acts 6:8–15

The crowd held its breath as the sixty-six-year-old tightrope walker inched his way across the wire, 750 feet in the air. Karl Wallenda was crossing Georgia's Tallulah Gorge, once again balancing on the edge of death.

Wallenda knew the pressure of walking the high wire. As the head of a large family that had been performing in circuses for years, he was constantly pushing the limits of human ability. Known as the Great Wallendas, his troupe of wire walkers had perfected hair-raising acts that thrilled audiences everywhere. Their most famous act was the seven-person pyramid, a stunt particularly phenomenal because they performed it without a net.

Why did Wallenda attempt such feats? He said his motivation was the people who flocked to see him—the audience. "They don't come to see you killed, but to see a man have the guts to face it," he said. "And maybe our act gives them a little courage to carry on in something themselves."[1]

Modeling a courage that inspires us to carry on is Stephen, the central figure in this chapter. He was just an ordinary Christian who had the vision to push the limits of faith—to step onto the high wire, trusting in God alone. And like Wallenda, who died at age seventy-three when he fell from a wire in San Juan, Puerto Rico, Stephen died while doing what he loved most—testifying of Christ. He lived and died on the raw edge of faith.

Stephen's story emerges from a spiritual awakening in the Jerusalem church. Let's take a moment to review the context.

General State of the Church

Three characteristics of the early church were instrumental in developing a godly man like Stephen.

First, *the church was not perfect, but it was sensitive.* Our last lesson

1. Karl Wallenda, as quoted by Richard Boeth in "The Fall of the Great Wallenda," *Newsweek*, April 3, 1978, p. 38.

illustrated one of the imperfections of the rapidly growing church: the Hellenistic widows had been overlooked in the distribution of food. The church corrected the problem by choosing seven Hellenistic men to oversee the benevolence ministry (Acts 6:1–5). Among these original deacons of the church was "Stephen, a man full of faith and of the Holy Spirit" (v. 5). Early on, the church recognized Stephen's character.

Second, *the church was not worldwide, but it was growing.* Still confined to Jerusalem, the church had yet to touch the world with the gospel. Nevertheless, it was growing, and "the number of the disciples continued to increase greatly in Jerusalem" (v. 7b). It was like a river about to overflow its banks.

Third, *the church was not endorsed, but it was effective.* "This new religion is strange," the temple priests must have commented to one another. Indeed, Christianity was unusual. It contained the transforming power of the Spirit and the living vitality of the risen Christ.

Out of this context, God zoomed in on one individual who epitomized the infectious spirit of the early church. As a model, Stephen showed us how to live true to the Lord despite external pressure—how to stay balanced when we find ourselves on the wire with no safety net below.

Specific Ministry of Stephen

As one of the chosen seven, Stephen's ministry included caring for needy believers. But this was only a portion of his spiritual contribution to the church. As we shall see, he expressed his faith and courage in other areas as well. Let's follow Stephen's story through the rest of Acts 6, and then in the next lesson, through chapter 7.

Name

The name *Stephen* comes from the Greek word *stephanos*, which means "a crown." In the Greek culture, it was

> the wreath, garland or chaplet given as a prize for victory, as a festal ornament, or as a public honour for distinguished service or personal worth.[2]

Such a name was fitting for Stephen, who distinguished himself

2. G. Abbott-Smith, *A Manual Greek Lexicon of the New Testament*, 3d ed. (Edinburgh, Scotland: T. & T. Clark, 1937), p. 27.

as a man of high spiritual acclaim and later would wear the honored crown of a martyr.

Reputation

Luke records that Stephen was "full of grace and power" (6:8a). Every aspect of his life overflowed with Christ's graciousness and the Spirit's power. "He was a released man," writes Lloyd Ogilvie.

> Defensiveness, self-justification, and competitiveness were gone. Graciousness became the discernible trait of his personality. He had the disposition of Christ. Faith had gotten him started, grace had kept him growing, and power was the result.[3]

He was balanced—tender yet tough, gracious yet strong. As a result, the power of the Holy Spirit worked through him mightily.

Miracles

Stephen performed "great wonders and signs among the people" (v. 8b). Through these miracles, God marked Stephen as one of His special messengers, even though he wasn't an apostle.

We would imagine that such a rare, unspoiled person was liked by everyone. But as verse 9 opens, a cloud of opposition appears, foreshadowing trouble ahead for Stephen.

Angry Reaction of the People

Antagonism toward Stephen came from the Synagogue of the Freedman and from the Sanhedrin. These two groups of religious leaders rained on Stephen torrents of contempt, testing his faith.

The Synagogue

Stephen's first trouble comes one day while he is preaching about Christ.

> Some men from what was called the Synagogue of the Freedmen,[4] including both Cyrenians and Alex-

3. Lloyd John Ogilvie, *Drumbeat of Love* (Waco, Tex.: Word Books, 1976), p. 88.

4. The Synagogue of the Freedmen consisted of Jews from foreign countries who were "once slaves of Rome (perhaps descendants of the Jews taken to Rome as captives by Pompey), now set free and settled in Jerusalem." Archibald Thomas Robertson, *Word Pictures in the New Testament* (Grand Rapids, Mich.: Baker Book House, 1930), vol. 3, p. 75.

andrians, and some from Cilicia and Asia, rose up
and argued with Stephen. (v. 9)

Like Stephen, these men were Hellenists, and one of them may
have been Paul, still called Saul at this time. Since his hometown,
Tarsus, was in Cilicia, he probably joined himself with other synagogue members from Cilicia. In fact, Saul may have instigated the
attack on Stephen—an attack that began simply as an argument.

Argumentation. Interrupting Stephen's sermon, the Pharisees
from the synagogue rise up and argue with him (see v. 9b). They
dispute what he is saying in the same way earlier Pharisees had
resisted Jesus' words. How easy it would be to fall to their level, to
wrangle and quarrel with them.

Notice, however, Stephen's response to this unexpected pressure. Although the Jews take the offensive,

they were unable to cope with the wisdom and the
Spirit with which he was speaking. (v. 10)

Calmly and graciously, he fended off their attacks. Luke never
tells us Stephen was an especially gifted speaker; he does say, though,
that Stephen was Spirit-filled. That was the reason for his eloquence.

His ability reminds us of what Jesus said to His disciples:

"They will lay their hands on you and will persecute
you, delivering you to the synagogues and prisons,
bringing you before kings and governors for My
name's sake. It will lead to an opportunity for your
testimony. So make up your minds not to prepare
beforehand to defend yourselves; for I will give you
utterance and wisdom which none of your opponents
will be able to resist or refute." (Luke 21:12–15)

When persecution struck, Jesus spoke through Stephen. And
when arrows fly your way, He will speak through you as well. Retaliating in the flesh will only lead to defeat; instead, depend on
His voice for words and for wisdom.

False accusations. Unable to cope with Stephen in direct confrontation, the Jewish leaders' next tactic is subterfuge.

They secretly induced men to say, "We have heard
him speak blasphemous words against Moses and
against God." And they stirred up the people, the

elders and the scribes. (Acts 6:11–12a)

The words *secretly induced* are translated from the Greek word *hupoballō*, which means "to put under like a carpet, to bring men under one's control by suggestion or by money."[5] With a few under-the-table deals, the Machiavellian religious leaders pay off some men to accuse Stephen of things he's never done. The lies and rumors grapevine quickly through the milling crowd.

Violence. Previously, the religious leaders had dared not man-handle the Christians for fear of the crowds (see 5:26). Now, because of the rumors, no one protested when "they came upon [Stephen] and dragged him away, and brought him before the Council" (6:12b).

Shouting and gloating, the officials shove innocent Stephen before the revenge-hungry Sanhedrin, who have been waiting for just this moment.

The Sanhedrin

Shamed by the reports of the risen Christ and embarrassed twice by Peter and the other apostles, the Sanhedrin eyes Stephen with disdain. All they need to convict him is a trumped-up case, and their judgment will be swift. The Jews from the synagogue provide their case.

> They put forward false witnesses who said, "This man incessantly speaks against this holy place, and the Law; for we have heard him say that this Nazarene, Jesus, will destroy this place and alter the customs which Moses handed down to us." (vv. 13–14)

Once again paralleling Jesus' experience before the Council, Stephen's story reveals two more pressure tactics taken by his enemies.

Exaggeration. The false witnesses say, "This man *incessantly* speaks against this holy place and the Law." Did Stephen really speak incessantly, without interruption? Attempting to legitimize their complaints, the accusers resort to a common ploy: "He *never* speaks about anything else; he *always* cuts down the temple and the Law." Their tactics don't stop with exaggeration, though.

Misrepresentation. In his sermon, Stephen apparently quoted

5. Robertson, *Word Pictures*, p. 76.

Jesus, who had said, "Destroy this temple, and in three days I will raise it up" (John 2:19). But in that context, Jesus "was speaking of the temple of His body" (v. 21). He was prophesying His own death and resurrection, the basis of the gospel message.

The false witnesses say Stephen claimed that Jesus would "destroy this place and alter the customs."[6] But they distorted his meaning, which was that Christ *fulfilled* Moses' law—His once-and-for-all sacrifice on the cross rendered the temple sacrifices useless.

Undeniable Impact of His Life

When the tirade finally quiets, all eyes turn toward Stephen,

> and fixing their gaze on him, all who were sitting in
> the Council saw his face like the face of an angel.[7]
> (Acts 6:15)

No clenched fists, no tightened lips, no grim stare. As he stands on that wire, with death on either side, God's undeniable peace shines from his face.

In the next lesson, we'll conclude Stephen's story. For now, we'll leave him with his face aglow, testifying to the amazing presence of God in his life. How can we have this same kind of peace under pressure? By reminding ourselves, first of all, that when we walk with Christ, the public will resent it, not support it. And second, when we react like Christ, the pressure will increase, not decrease.

And most important, when we rely on Christ's strength, God's peace will pervade in the midst of angry shouts and false accusations. Francis R. Havergal described this peace in his hymn "Like a River Glorious":

> Hidden in the hollow
> Of His blessed hand,
> Never foe can follow
> Never traitor stand;
> Not a surge of worry,

---

6. The false witnesses at Jesus' trial used this same tactic to accuse Him and even the same misquote: "Two came forward, and said, '[Jesus] stated, "I am able to destroy the temple of God and to rebuild it in three days."'" (Matt. 26:60b–61)

7. Stephen's face shone like Moses' had after he had been with the Lord (Exod. 34:30). Ironically, the Council accused Stephen of opposing Moses, but he was more like Moses than any of them.

Not a shade of care,
Not a blast of hurry
    Touch the Spirit there.
Stayed upon Jehovah,
    Hearts are fully blest;
Finding, as He promised,
    Perfect peace and rest.[8]

 ## Living Insights

With a shove, you're out on the wire. Can't step back; your accusers are ready to push you out again, breathlessly eager to see you fall. Can't look down; the ground swirls below, making you dizzy. You squeeze your eyes shut. "Balance," you tell yourself, *"balance!"*

To cross this tightrope safely, reflect for a moment on how Stephen maintained his balance. What character traits helped him stay balanced (see especially Acts 6:5 and 8a)?

_____

_____

_____

_____

Right now you may be enduring the pressure of a lawsuit, a family fight, or a job-related fracas in which others are blaming you and spreading rumors. How can emulating Stephen's character guide you safely across your tightrope of trouble?

_____

_____

_____

_____

8. Frances R. Havergal, "Like a River Glorious," from *Inspiring Hymns*, comp. Alfred B. Smith (Grand Rapids, Mich.: Zondervan Publishing House, Singspiration, 1968), no. 485.

Stephen's experience mirrors Jesus' run-in with Jerusalem's religious leaders in several ways. Both men were accused of the same crimes by false witnesses. They both raised the ire of the Sanhedrin, and both suffered unjustly. If anyone could understand Stephen's feelings during his ordeal, it was Jesus.

Jesus understands your feelings as well. He understands when people viciously tear you apart with their words, when exaggerations turn friends against you. He knows what it is like to be locked out by others, with despair your only companion.

At these times Jesus is near. Climb into His lap and discover His comfort.

> Since then we have a great high priest who has passed through the heavens, Jesus the Son of God, let us hold fast our confession. For we do not have a high priest who cannot sympathize with our weaknesses, but one who has been tempted in all things as we are, yet without sin. Let us therefore draw near with confidence to the throne of grace, that we may receive mercy and may find grace to help in time of need. (Heb. 4:14–16)

Use the following space to draw near to Jesus, expressing your concerns and fears to Him.

_____

_____

_____

_____

_____

_____

_____

_____

Chapter 15

A COURAGEOUS SWAN SONG

Acts 7

The buildings have weathered, the weeds have grown high, but at certain places where history was made, nothing really changes. In the British House of Commons, Winston Churchill's growl still echoes through the chambers. At Gettysburg, Abraham Lincoln's "Fourscore and seven years ago" still rings clear. In locations like these, the voices of the past seem to drift in the wind, filling the air with a nostalgic sacredness.

One of those voices floats across time to us in Acts 7. It belongs to Stephen, the first martyr of the church. No monument marks the place where he made his final stand—only his words remain for a memorial. So as we examine these words, imagine yourself standing where he spoke them. Hear the echo. Feel the passion. For the lines were born from the courageous heart of a man prepared to die.

Accusation and Question

In our last lesson we learned that Stephen had been performing miracles and preaching the gospel. This offended some of the synagogue Jews, who began spreading lies and persuading a few men to give false witness against him (Acts 6:8–11). When they dragged him before the Sanhedrin, the Supreme Court of the Jews, the accusation rang out: "This man incessantly speaks against this holy place, and the Law" (v. 13b). Dressed in their robes of sophistication, the seventy Council members glared while they pelted him with charges, one after the other.

Finally, the high priest, the same man who had condemned Jesus, asked Stephen, "Are these things so?" (7:1a). Had he blasphemed Moses and God? Had he ridiculed the temple and the Law?

Stephen answers these allegations in a speech that covers fifty-three verses and two thousand years of Jewish history. It is a speech that binds the Hebrew Scriptures with a single theme, a scarlet cord—Jesus.

117

Declaration and Review

Although we will touch only the highlights, Luke records this lengthy sermon in its entirety because of its significance to the case of Christianity. In it, Stephen, the great apologist, defends and glorifies Jesus and speaks with two purposes in mind.

Purpose of the Message

His first purpose is to answer with facts the charges against him. Because he has been accused of being a blasphemer, Stephen speaks highly of God, Moses, and the temple, using Scripture in every point he makes (for examples, see Acts 7:36–38, 47–50). As R. C. H. Lenski reflects, "What could be blasphemous about a man who spoke as reverently and as Biblically as this man did?"[1]

Second, Stephen endeavors to confront sin with the truth. He reminded them that the Scriptures taught that a prophet like Moses would appear—a prophet known as the Messiah (v. 37). The Scriptures also said that God would not dwell in a temple made by hands (v. 48). Jesus, Stephen concludes, is the fulfillment of the Old Testament prophecies. The Jewish leaders, however, have sinned because they have rejected Christ and disobeyed God.

Disobedience versus obedience, belief versus unbelief—these are the resounding themes of the message. Like drum taps, they reverberate softly at first. Abraham, Joseph, and Moses obeyed God; Joseph's brothers and the Israelites in the wilderness disobeyed God. The themes crescendo steadily, until the beat has become a deafening indictment. The self-righteous Sanhedrin members are *not* part of believing Israel; they are like their fathers—unrighteous, unbelieving Israel.

As we analyze the specifics of Stephen's message, we discover that it encompasses these themes in a broad survey of the Old Testament.

Analysis of the Survey

Stephen's survey emphasizes God's relationship with the Jews, beginning with Abraham in Genesis and ending with the prophets. The following chart outlines the six subjects in his sermon and the corresponding Old Testament books.

---

1. R. C. H. Lenski, *The Interpretation of the Acts of the Apostles* (Columbus, Ohio: Wartburg Press, 1944), p. 259.

Sermon Reference	Subject	Old Testament Book(s)
Acts 7:2–16	God selected and directed our fathers	Genesis
vv. 17–41	God protected and freed our fathers	Exodus to Leviticus
vv. 42–44	God tested and instructed our fathers	Numbers to Deuteronomy
v. 45	God conquered and gave land to our fathers	Joshua to 1 Samuel
vv. 46–47	God met with and blessed our fathers	2 Samuel to 2 Chronicles
vv. 48–50	God communicated with our fathers	Ezra to Malachi

God selected and directed our fathers (Acts 7:2–16). By faith, Abraham followed God's call to an unknown land. God promised that his offspring would possess the land and enjoy His protection (vv. 2–7). From Abraham's son Isaac to Isaac's son Jacob, the covenant then passed to Jacob's twelve sons, "the twelve patriarchs" (v. 8b). But

> the patriarchs became jealous of Joseph [their brother] and sold him into Egypt. And yet God was with him, and rescued him from all his afflictions, and granted him favor and wisdom in the sight of Pharaoh, king of Egypt; and he made him governor over Egypt and all his household. (vv. 9–10)

Joseph later reunited his family and they came to live with him in Egypt. Four hundred years later, Moses was born.

God protected and freed our fathers (vv. 17–41). By this time the Hebrews were slaves in Egypt. God chose Moses to free them, but the Israelites had previously rejected Moses, who then fled Egypt (vv. 17–30a). When God brought him back as their deliverer, they continued to grumble against Him, even though He led them out of bondage (vv. 30b–38).

"Our fathers," Stephen comments, "were unwilling to be obedient to him, but repudiated him and in their hearts turned back to Egypt" (v. 39). They even made a golden calf and worshiped it instead of God (v. 41). As a result, the next period in Israel's history was a time of testing.

God tested and instructed our fathers (vv. 42–44). Moses built a portable worship center called the tabernacle. As the Hebrews traversed the wilderness, God was with them, instructing them. But, quoting the prophet Amos, Stephen reminds his audience that the Hebrews still sinned by taking "along the tabernacle of Moloch and the star of the god Rompha" (v. 43).

He continues with Israel's record of unbelief by quickly surveying the next three periods.

God conquered and gave land to our fathers (v. 45). In one verse, Stephen covers the conquest of Canaan and the division of the land among the twelve tribes of Israel.

God met with and blessed our fathers (vv. 46–47). Stephen proceeds to King David and his son Solomon, who received God's blessing because of their faith. Though Solomon built the permanent temple for God to indwell, Isaiah had stated that God would not be limited to a building.

God communicated with our fathers (vv. 48–50). Through Isaiah's prophecy, Stephen passionately explains what God communicated to His people:

> "'Heaven is My throne,
> And earth is the footstool of My feet;
> What kind of house will you build for Me?' says
> the Lord;
> 'Or what place is there for My repose?
> Was it not My hand which made all these
> things?'"
> (vv. 49–50)

"God is bigger than this temple or this Council," Stephen is saying. Now the stage is set to reveal the religious leaders' sin—their rejection of the God of heaven, His Son, and His sovereign plan.

Confrontation and Death

Throughout his sermon, Stephen has repeated the phrases, "our father" or "our fathers," including himself as a Jewish descendant.[2]

2. The phrase "our father(s)" occurs nine times in the sermon, in verses 2, 12, 15, 19, 38, 39, 44, and 45.

Now, having illustrated the insidious unbelief of their forefathers, he changes the phrase to "*your* fathers." In so doing, as Lenski observes, he "turns the tables completely by putting accusers, witnesses, and court itself on the hopeless defense."[3]

The leaders accuse him of blasphemy, but they are the blasphemers. They accuse him of rejecting Moses, who received the Law; but they are rejecting the true Prophet, Jesus, who fulfilled the Law.

With teeth bared, the Council members crouch like wounded tigers. Seeing death in their hateful eyes, Stephen concludes with all his heart:

> "You men who are stiff-necked and uncircumcised in heart and ears are always resisting the Holy Spirit; you are doing just as your fathers did. Which one of the prophets did your fathers not persecute? And they killed those who had previously announced the coming of the Righteous One, whose betrayers and murderers you have now become; you who received the law as ordained by angels, and yet did not keep it." (vv. 51–53)

The events that follow tumble over each other in heated succession. Boiling emotions explode, violent anger erupts, and Stephen is left dead. In the midst of this horror, God teaches us three valuable lessons.

When Confronted with Sin, the Religious Are Enraged . . . Not Receptive

Stephen was hardly able to spout out his last words before the leaders were on him. "They were cut to the quick, and they began gnashing their teeth at him" (v. 54). Seventy enraged men

> cried out with a loud voice, and covered their ears, and they rushed upon him with one impulse. And when they had driven him out of the city, they began stoning him. (vv. 57–58a)

When Death Is Near, the Lord Offers Courage . . . Not Necessarily Escape

The Lord's courage allowed Stephen to accept his death. Before

3. Lenski, *Acts of the Apostles*, p. 259.

Stephen was stoned, Luke tells us,

> being full of the Holy Spirit, he gazed intently into
> heaven and saw the glory of God, and Jesus standing
> at the right hand of God; and he said, "Behold, I see
> the heavens opened up and the Son of Man standing
> at the right hand of God." (vv. 55–56)

In his vision, Stephen saw Jesus standing, not sitting—as if to
say, "Come home, son."

As the stones pounded his flesh, "he called upon the Lord and
said, 'Lord Jesus, receive my spirit!'" (v. 59). Then, with amazing
fortitude and courageous love, he fell to his knees and

> cried out with a loud voice, "Lord, do not hold this
> sin against them!" And having said this, he fell
> asleep. (v. 60)

When Separated from This Life, the Christian Is Welcomed Home . . . Not Rejected

In an instant, Stephen was home. Maligned and mistreated on
earth, he was eagerly embraced by the Lord of heaven. This same
welcome awaits all who bear His name—who stand beneath the
Cross, who wait beside the tomb, who follow Stephen's path.

Living Insights

Death is a formidable enemy. Can we muster the courage to
face it?

In a sermon titled "Heaven," the late evangelist Billy Sunday
helps fortify our hearts by reminding us of our enemy's weakness.

> Death is a cruel enemy. He robs the mother of
> her baby, the wife of her husband, the parents of
> their children, the lover of his intended wife. . . .
>
> Death is a rude enemy. He upsets our best plans
> without an apology. He enters the most exclusive
> circles without an invitation.
>
> Death is an international enemy. There is no
> nation which he does not visit. The islands of the
> seas where . . . mothers rock their babies to sleep
> to the lullaby of the ocean's waves. The restless sea.

The majestic mountains. All are his haunts.

Death is an untiring enemy. He continues his ghastly work Spring, Summer, Autumn and Winter. He never tires in his ceaseless rounds, gathering his spoils of human souls.

But Death is a vanquished enemy. Jesus arose from the dead and abolished death. . . .

Death to the Christian is swinging open the door through which he passes into Heaven.[4]

Christ proved His victory over death when He opened heaven and showed Himself to Stephen in a vision. This image assured the martyr that it was true, that Jesus had vanquished the foe.

For further assurance of death's defeat, read 1 Corinthians 15:50–58. How do Paul's words give you the courage to face death?

Because Christ has disarmed death, we can refuse to live in its shadow. How does Paul advise us to live instead (see 1 Cor. 15:58)?

In what ways can you follow his advice today?

Though our bodies decay, death's power is limited. Do not fear! Christ has won the battle.

---

4. Billy Sunday, as quoted by Lyle W. Dorsett in *Billy Sunday and the Redemption of Urban America* (Grand Rapids, Mich.: William B. Eerdmans Publishing Co., 1991), p. 173.

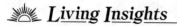

The religious leaders may have thrown stones at Stephen, but it was the truth they really stoned—the truth of their own failure, their own sin. In Stephen's words they saw a reflection of their depravity. So, rather than accept the pain, they smashed the mirror.

How hard it is for us as well to face the truth about ourselves. It irritates us. It enrages us. It terrifies us. What truth about yourself angers you? Some fault? Some habitual sin? Some inadequacy?

The target of our flailing tirade may be someone as innocent as Stephen—a parent, a spouse, a friend, a sibling, a child, even God Himself. Has someone close to you been damaged by your prideful anger? If so, whom? How did you hurt them?

In the midst of our stone throwing, however, the sweet words of Stephen rise above the onslaught: "Lord, do not hold this sin against them!" (Acts 7:60b). Christ offers forgiveness for our anger and for our deepest sin.

Do you need to ask forgiveness from someone you've hurt with your anger? In the space provided, express your words in a letter. Then share these words with that person as soon as you can.

Chapter 16

THE PURE AND
THE PHONY
Acts 8:1–24

C hances are, most of us will never know what it means to be persecuted. The worst kind of persecution we endure is a little mockery at school, a little sarcasm at the office, or a little trouble in the neighborhood. Yet often, these things just paralyze us for weeks, don't they?

How revealing it would be if such persecution as the early Christians endured suddenly came upon us. That's when we'd move from the realm of theory to reality. At that moment our faith would either stand or fall because persecution always separates the pure from the phony, the authentic from the artificial. Always.

Now we've reached a turning point in our study of Acts. As we learned in the first lesson, Acts 1–7 covers the establishment of the church in Jerusalem. For two years the believers have been involved in "city evangelism." Chapter 8 begins a new phase: the church scattered to Judea and Samaria. The catalyst that pushed Christianity beyond Jerusalem's borders? Persecution. And through this suffering, God separated the pure from the phony.

Martyrdom Ignites Persecution

Stephen's stoning unleashed a torrent of violence against the Jewish believers. At the helm of that violence was a man named Saul. Luke gives us a brief glimpse of him.

> The witnesses laid aside their robes at the feet of a young man named Saul. . . . And Saul was in hearty agreement with putting [Stephen] to death.
> And on that day a great persecution arose against the church in Jerusalem. . . . Saul began ravaging the church, entering house after house; and dragging off men and women, he would put them in prison. (Acts 7:58b; 8:1–2a, 3)

Saul determined to destroy Christianity through persecution. Later, he recalled the extent of his ravaging: "I persecuted this Way to the death, binding and putting both men and women into prisons" (22:4). He went on: "In one synagogue after another I used to imprison and beat those who believed" (v. 19b, see also 26:9–11).

In Gestapo fashion, he imprisoned, tortured, and murdered. Amazingly, Saul would soon become Paul, the champion of the gospel and author of much of the New Testament. But for now, the believers groaned under his crushing assault, wondering whether Stephen's end would be their fate too.

Such persecution could have smothered the flame of Christ. Instead, like pouring gasoline on a burning match, the suffering fueled a fire that exploded into even greater evangelism!

Persecution Prompts True Evangelism

Until now, the gospel had penetrated only Jerusalem. But Christ had a much broader plan for His salvation message.

Predicted by Christ

Let's return to Christ's plan in the first chapter of Acts and look again at His words to the apostles:

> You shall be My witnesses both in Jerusalem, and in
> all Judea and Samaria, and even to the remotest part
> of the earth. (v. 8b)

The first phase of operation was being accomplished; as Luke records in chapter 6: "the number of the disciples continued to increase greatly in Jerusalem" (v. 7b). But God has a heart for the world, and now it was time to expand to the next circle of influence. Persecution, therefore, became the splash in the pond to send the gospel rippling outward.

Experienced by Christians

Suffering sent many of the Christians into regions they never thought they would enter. One such place was Samaria.[1] What did they do there?

Luke tells us that "those who had been scattered went about preaching the word" (8:4). Their preaching was effective, too, as evidenced by Philip's story in verses 5–8. You recall Philip; along

---

1. The Jewish believers may have initially balked at taking the gospel to Samaria because, as John explains in his gospel, "Jews have no dealings with Samaritans" (4:9b).

with Stephen, he was one of the seven deacons chosen to distribute food to the needy. Since then, his ministry had grown beyond Jerusalem and he had become an evangelist. In his ministry, we can isolate three characteristics that produced what we'll call true evangelism.

First, true evangelism emphasizes the *centrality of Jesus*. Philip went to the city of Samaria and "began proclaiming Christ to them" (8:5b). His ministry shone with integrity, because the focus was Jesus, not a person or a program.

Philip's ministry also had a *dynamic of liberating power*. Multitudes, Luke reports, believed Philip's message because they

> heard and saw the signs which he was performing. For in the case of many who had unclean spirits, they were coming out of them shouting with a loud voice; and many who had been paralyzed and lame were healed. (vv. 6–7)

Through these miracles, God confirmed Philip as His man and Philip's message as His Word. The ministry was pure because it exhibited an unexplainable power that was changing lives, not merely drawing crowds.

Finally, Philip's evangelism included the *presence of contagious joy*. According to the account, "there was much rejoicing in that city" (v. 8). They were having fun! Laughter and joy filled the streets because the townspeople were experiencing the rapture of a relationship with God through Christ.

Where Christ is, there is joy. But Christ is not in all ministries; unfortunately, some are phony. One such false ministry arose in Samaria alongside Philip's and was centered around a man named Simon.

True Evangelism Exposes False Faith

A rhinestone may sparkle, but when compared to a diamond, its flaws are exposed. In the same way, Philip's true evangelism revealed the glaring defects in Simon's ministry. If you look carefully, you can see five of them.

Characteristics of the Phony

The first sure sign of a phony ministry is found in verse 9.

> Now there was a certain man named Simon, who

formerly was practicing magic in the city, and astonishing the people of Samaria, claiming to be someone great.

Philip proclaimed Christ; Simon proclaimed himself. The principle characteristic of a phony faith is that it *exalts a person rather than Christ.*

The second characteristic of Simon's act was that he was *drawing a following based on fleshly attractions and impressions.* He was running a circus! Look at what the people called him in verse 10:

> And they all, from smallest to greatest, were giving attention to him, saying, "This man is what is called the Great Power of God."

We can almost hear the sideshow barker announcing: "Come see Simon the Magnificent and his astounding acts of God!"[2] Simon was a manipulator and a deceiver. And his astounding acts were certainly not of God.

> And they were giving him attention because he had for a long time astonished them with his magic arts. (v. 11)

From this verse, we recognize the third sign of a phony ministry: *exercising counterfeit power.* Like Pharaoh's magicians in Moses' day, Simon performed supernatural feats with the power of darkness (see Exod. 7:8–13; 20–22). His magic arts were not mere illusions; more likely, they were demonic acts disguised as God's miracles.

His show earned him a large following, but when Philip came and performed God-empowered miracles, Simon's abilities paled in comparison. Even he recognized God's power and soon professed faith in Christ (see Acts 8:12–13).

But Simon's conversion was not genuine. He just wanted an inside look at this new spiritual power without becoming too personally involved. He was manifesting the fourth characteristic of phony faith: *going through the religious motions for the wrong motives.*

At this point, even Philip may have thought that Simon's conversion was real. But when Peter and John arrived from Jerusalem,

---

2. In contrast to Simon's phoniness, the apostle Paul later exhibited humble honesty in his ministry to the Corinthians: "I was with you in weakness and in fear and in much trembling" (1 Cor. 2:3).

Simon's true nature became clear. The two apostles came to lay hands on the Samaritan believers and pray that they would receive the Holy Spirit, "for He had not yet fallen upon any of them" (v. 16a).[3] On the side, Simon was watching.

> When Simon saw that the Spirit was bestowed through the laying on of the apostles' hands, he offered them money, saying, "Give this authority to me as well, so that everyone on whom I lay my hands may receive the Holy Spirit." (vv. 18–19)

His request betrayed his heart and illustrated the final characteristic of a false faith: *preoccupation with the material rather than the spiritual.* Interested in its profit-making potential, he hoped he could purchase God's power. But one can't buy God, a fact Peter quickly pointed out.

Confrontation by the Pure

Perceiving Simon's hypocrisy, Peter immediately called him to task:

> "May your silver perish with you, because you thought you could obtain the gift of God with money! You have no part or portion in this matter, for your heart is not right before God. Therefore repent of this wickedness of yours, and pray the Lord that if possible, the intention of your heart may be forgiven you. For I see that you are in the gall of bitterness and in the bondage of iniquity." (vv. 20–23)

Simon's response may have sounded humble, but a tone of sarcastic stubbornness seeped through.

> "Pray to the Lord for me yourselves, so that nothing of what you have said may come upon me." (v. 24)

---

3. The delay allowed those who first received the Spirit to deliver the message. This transitional period required a special induction of these new Samaritan believers. "This was calculated to remove any sense of inferiority and to encourage them to feel their oneness with others in the body of Christ." Everett F. Harrison, *Interpreting Acts* (Grand Rapids, Mich.: Zondervan Publishing House, Academie Books, 1986), p. 146.

Application for Today

Persecution, as difficult as it was to endure, was God's tool to separate the pure from the phony in the early church. He also used it to push the gospel message farther out from Jerusalem, as chased and tormented Christians took Christ's flame with them to new lands.

If you are going through suffering, let it do its heart surgery to cut away the phoniness in your life. Let it purify Christ's message of freedom and joy. Then let others see the tested and proven gospel in your life, wherever you go.

☀ *Living Insights*

Suffering separates the pure from the phony. As long as Christianity is comfortable, the church will be filled with false believers. Apply a dose of persecution, and only the true followers of Christ will remain.

Do you know whether you would stay true to Jesus if tested? The three marks of true evangelism we studied will give you a measure to evaluate your staying power.

First, is Christ central to your life? Do you talk with Him in prayer? Do you talk about Him with others? Does His will for you supersede your own?

_____

_____

_____

Second, are you experiencing the liberating power of the gospel? Do you feel bound to a religious system? Have you sensed a release from your former sinful lifestyle? Has the Holy Spirit's power been evident in your life?

_____

_____

_____

Third, how has Christ's joy filled your life? Has His peace settled on your heart? Has His love resolved disharmonies with others?

_____

_____

_____

If these characteristics are a little dull in your life, how can you polish them up so that when persecution comes you'll be prepared?

• The centrality of Jesus Christ: _____

_____

_____

_____

• The dynamic of liberating power: _____

_____

_____

_____

• The presence of contagious joy: _____

_____

_____

_____

🔆 *Living Insights* STUDY TWO

Like lost prodigals coming home, the Samaritans embraced Christ's message of forgiveness (Acts 8:6–8). David Redding's reflections on the parable of the prodigal (Luke 15:11–32) describe how the people must have felt.

> The returning prodigal was absolutely bewildered . . . by his father's reckless forgiveness and extravagant love. When he was so utterly lost and alone,

he was found. At the end of his rope, at last he came into an incredible kingdom. The fattest calf, the warmest coat, and the costliest ring were his. "There was the sound of music and dancing."[4]

Like the father of the prodigal, Jesus also loves us extravagantly. Realizing this, Redding exclaims, "I tell you—Jesus makes me laugh." Have you ever felt like the returning prodigal? Does the thought of Jesus' lavish grace thrill you? Does Jesus make you laugh?

Sometimes life's craziness can bury your Christian joy. If it has been a while since you've laughed—or even smiled—at the thought of Jesus' love, how can you resurrect the joy of the Lord inside you? You may want to fill your home with Christian music, talk about Jesus with a neighbor, or focus more on worship at church. What are your ideas?

_____

_____

_____

_____

_____

_____

_____

4. David A. Redding, *Jesus Makes Me Laugh with Him* (Grand Rapids, Mich.: Zondervan Publishing House, 1977), p. 103.

Chapter 17

GOD'S WAY OF WINNING
Acts 8:25–40

Most Christians would rather do almost anything than witness.
There are a number of reasons for this feeling. One is ignorance
—we don't really know how to go about it. Another is indifference.
We have other things to think about, after all, and besides, there
are plenty of evangelists out there doing the job better than we
could. We're perfectly willing to pick up the tab if they'll do the
work. Still another reason we're reluctant is fear. Nobody likes being
made a fool of or being asked questions they can't answer. And what
if the response is hostile? The whole idea is just too scary.

Also, some of us have an unpleasant memory of a bad experience
when someone grabbed us by the collar and shoved the gospel down
our throat. We remember that embarrassed, intruded-upon, pres-
sured feeling, and the last thing we want to do is make someone
else feel that way.

We know we should share our faith, but we still feel awkward.
"A lot of us just don't know how to approach people," writes Paul
Little.

> Though we've built up a head of steam, we're still
> preparing for that great tomorrow that's never
> come. We're like the enthusiastic coach, inspiring his
> team in the locker room, "Here we are undefeated,
> untied, unscored upon . . . and ready for our first
> game!" We've never risked spoiling our record by
> going out to face the opposition.[1]

Yet God yearns for us to get into the game. He has chosen us
to be His voice, to introduce lost people to the most exciting message they will ever hear. So in the next few pages, let's discuss our
game plan—how to win people for Christ, God's way.

This lesson is based on "Strengthening Your Grip on Evangelism" in the study guide *Strengthening Your Grip*, coauthored by Ken Gire, from the Bible-teaching ministry of Charles R.
Swindoll (Fullerton, Calif.: Insight for Living, 1989).

1. Paul E. Little, *How to Give Away Your Faith* (Downers Grove, Ill.: InterVarsity Press,
1966), pp. 23–24.

Various Approaches to Winning Souls

Some strategies for witnessing don't work very well. Christians who use the "Eager Beaver Approach," for instance, blurt out the gospel to any and everybody, regardless of the situation. They stack up converts as if they were cordwood, and the higher the pile, the better they look. This gnawing, decision-centered approach gets results and relieves guilt—you

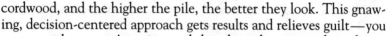

know you've witnessed that day—but it is rude and usually offends unbelievers, chilling them to the gospel.

Then there is the "Ivy League Approach." This strategy is reason-centered and intellectual. "Let's discuss world religions," the philosophical witness may say. Although this approach is open and respectful, it rarely mentions sin or our need for God's forgiveness. It is too vague.

The next method is the "Mute Approach." "I'm a silent witness for God," says this Christian. Never offensive, never challenging, this witness follows Christ but never invites anyone else to come along. This is a lopsided approach; living the gospel without explaining it is like trying to fly an airplane with only one wing—you will never get off the ground.

In this lesson's Scripture passage, we'll see the biblical approach. This game plan emphasizes putting ourselves in the other person's place. By taking this tack, you'll perceive the underlying needs of others; and you'll realize that they essentially want four things from you:

1. They want to see what's inside you—the real you.

2. They want to know that you are listening to them.

3. They want you to scratch them, spiritually speaking, where they itch.

4. They want you to talk *with* them, not *at* them.

Our model for this winning strategy will be Philip, the Billy Graham of the first century. But don't let that description intimidate you—he was a layperson, like most of us, and the principles we find in his life relate to every Christian.

God's Preferred Guidelines

God had been using Philip to spearhead a dynamic evangelistic crusade in Samaria, spreading the gospel to many villages in the area (Acts 8:25). The work couldn't have been going better. But suddenly, God stepped in with an unexpected directive.

> An angel of the Lord spoke to Philip saying, "Arise and go south to the road that descends from Jerusalem to Gaza." (This is a desert road.) (v. 26)

Philip's response to this command illustrates the first guideline in God's witnessing game plan.

Sensitivity

Out of the blue, God tells Philip to take off for the desert. No reason is given. And no arrangements are made for someone to take his place in Samaria. There's just a command.

How tempting it would have been for him to brush that still, small voice away like a gnat buzzing in his ear. The ministry is going so well; the Samaritans are open to the gospel. But Philip had walked with God long enough to know that He has a reason for throwing us a curve now and then. He knew that to be an effective witness, he had to be sensitive to God's call.

Availability

Sensitivity has a Siamese twin—availability. There's not much good in hearing God's call if you're not willing to follow it when it comes.

> He arose and went; and behold, there was an Ethiopian eunuch, a court official of Candace, queen of the Ethiopians, who was in charge of all her treasure; and he had come to Jerusalem to worship.[2] And he

2. The phrase "and behold" is often used by Luke to emphasize sudden and providential interposition. Compare Acts 1:10; 10:17; and 12:7. See W. Robertson Nicoll, "The Acts of the Apostles," in *The Expositor's Greek Testament* (Grand Rapids, Mich.: William B. Eerdmans Publishing Co., n.d.), p. 222.

was returning and sitting in his chariot, and was reading the prophet Isaiah. (vv. 27–28)

Who would have thought it? Out there in the middle of nowhere is a political leader, riding in his chariot and reading the Word of God.[3] No one but God could have known how receptive this man was. Philip didn't know that this Ethiopian was the reason for his unexpected journey south. He simply was available to the Lord, who in His sovereign plan caused their paths to cross.

Initiative

Still obedient, Philip follows the Holy Spirit's direction.

And the Spirit said to Philip, "Go up and join this chariot." And when Philip had run up, he heard him reading Isaiah the prophet, and said, "Do you understand what you are reading?" (vv. 29–30)

Philip didn't wait for the man to lean out of his chariot and holler, "Excuse me, but do you happen to be an Old Testament scholar?" No, he took the initiative—but he took it with sensitivity. He didn't swagger up with his thumb in his suspender, toting his concordance under his arm. He didn't pull out his textbook on apologetics, ready for an argument. He wasn't out to impress or convince. He came graciously, with only one simple question: "Do you understand what you are reading?"

Tactfulness

Philip's question gets a straightforward answer.

"Well, how could I, unless someone guides me?" And he invited Philip to come up and sit with him. (v. 31)

Philip didn't charge up to the chariot, wielding answers. Instead, he waited for an invitation to come and share what he knew about the Scriptures. And before he spoke, he listened to the man.

Now the passage of Scripture which he was reading was this:
"He was led as a sheep to slaughter;

---

3. "Ethiopia" refers to "a large territory lying directly south of Egypt, hence to be distinguished from modern Ethiopia located to the southeast." Everett F. Harrison, *Interpreting Acts* (Grand Rapids, Mich.: Zondervan Publishing House, Academie Books, 1986), p. 150.

And as a lamb before its shearer is silent,
So He does not open His mouth.
In humiliation His judgment was taken away;
Who shall relate His generation?
For His life is removed from the earth."
And the eunuch answered Philip and said, "Please
tell me, of whom does the prophet say this? Of him-
self, or of someone else?" (vv. 32–34)

Philip's tactfulness paid off. The man asked a question that opened the door for the gospel message. Then it was natural for Philip to talk about Christ, the subject of Isaiah's prophecy.

Sometimes witnessing seems like such an unnatural act that to accomplish it we find ourselves acting in an unnatural manner. People who are ordinarily courteous and polite, people who know which fork to use when and how to carry on sociable small talk, suddenly become pushy and obnoxious.

Paul Little writes wryly about his early witnessing experiences in a way many of us can relate to.

> About once every six months the pressure to witness used to reach explosive heights inside me. Not know-ing any better, I would suddenly lunge at someone and spout all my verses with a sort of glazed stare in my eye. I honestly didn't expect any response. As soon as my victim indicated lack of interest, I'd begin to edge away from him with a sigh of relief and the consoling thought, "All that will live godly in Christ Jesus shall suffer persecution" (II Timothy 3:12). Duty done, I'd draw back into my martyr's shell for another six months' hibernation, until the internal pressure again became intolerable and drove me out. It really shocked me when I finally realized that I, not the cross, was offending people.[4]

Precision

With tact, Philip lets the man ask his questions without inter-ruption. With precision, he gives the answers.

4. Little, *How to Give Away Your Faith*, p. 32.

137

> Philip opened his mouth, and beginning from this
> Scripture he preached Jesus to him. (v. 35)

Even when questions sound stupid or heretical or even blasphemous, we should let them be asked. We should let people say what they need to say. Like Philip, we have to meet them on whatever road they're on and from there lead them to Calvary.

Philip didn't give the man any highfalutin philosophy; there's no record here of any "turn-or-burn" threats or scary charts about beasts and famines. There aren't even any irresistible promises of cloud-nine peace or answers to all of life's problems. There's just talk about Jesus—His perfect life and His sacrificial death. Philip didn't give the eunuch a course on Old Testament prophecy. He simply "preached Jesus."

It takes skill to avoid getting rabbit-trailed when you're witnessing. People have a remarkable ability to pull you off the subject and onto the pain of the world or the issue of evolution or the latest church scandal. But Jesus is truly the only issue that matters.

Decisiveness

Philip's witnessing game plan is working. The gospel message penetrates the man's heart to such an extent that

> as they went along the road they came to some water;
> and the eunuch said, "Look! Water! What prevents
> me from being baptized?" (v. 36)

At this point, Philip wisely puts first things first. Knowing that salvation comes through faith, not baptism, he says decisively, "If you believe with all your heart, you may." And the eunuch answered, "I believe that Jesus Christ is the Son of God" (see v. 37).[5]

> And he ordered the chariot to stop; and they both
> went down into the water, Philip as well as the eunuch; and he baptized him. (v. 38)

First there was a private acceptance of the message and then there was an outward demonstration of faith.

---

5. This exchange between Philip and the eunuch was not part of the original Bible text but was added later to clarify that the Ethiopian did believe in Christ before his baptism.

Following Up and Going On

Normally, in our witnessing strategy, the next step would be follow-up—spiritual guidance for the new believer. But in this situation, something startling happened.

> When they came up out of the water, the Spirit of the Lord snatched Philip away; and the eunuch saw him no more, but went on his way rejoicing. But Philip found himself at Azotus; and as he passed through he kept preaching the gospel to all the cities, until he came to Caesarea. (vv. 39–40)

With a snap of the fingers, Philip was gone. His job was finished, but the court official's mission was just beginning, for he carried the gospel flame back to the land of Ethiopia. Prophecy foretold the results: "Ethiopia will quickly stretch out her hands to God" (Ps. 68:31).

A nation embraces the gospel because Philip sensed God's leading, obeyed His command, tactfully talked about Jesus, and guided a certain man to believe. Could God be asking you to be like Philip, to follow his approach, to speak up about your faith? Maybe, so far, this has been an untried game for you. Perhaps you have a long list of reasons for staying on the bench . . . but the Coach is calling your name.

Go ahead, get in the game.

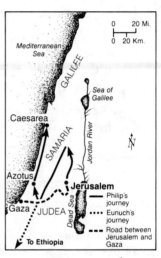

Philip's Ministry[6]

6. *Life Application® Bible*, New International Version (copublishers; Wheaton, Ill.: Tyndale House Publishers, 1991 and Grand Rapids, Mich.: Zondervan Publishing House, 1991), p. 1961. Maps © 1986, 1988 by Tyndale House Publishers, Inc. All rights reserved. Used by permission.

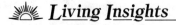

People everywhere are waiting on their own desert roads for us to show them Christ. Unfortunately, the sounds of our fast-paced city lives often drown out God's whisper of where they are. We need quiet moments with God so that He can communicate His leading to us. Paul Little wrote,

> Inner spiritual reality developed by a secret life with God is essential for an effective witness to a pagan world.[7]

But as John Stott, a renowned British minister, admitted:

> The thing I know will give me the deepest joy— namely, to be alone and unhurried in the presence of God, aware of His presence, my heart open to worship Him—is often the thing I least want to do.[8]

If you can identify with Stott's feelings, what would help you resolve this paradox and begin to have regular quiet times with God?

_____

_____

_____

Take a moment right now. With open Bible, reflect on the Scriptures in this lesson. Who is the searching Ethiopian in your life? Is God telling you where to find this person? What to say? Let God speak to you in the quietness.

God doesn't have to send you out to the desert to meet searching people. They may be right in your neighborhood, even next door. But many times we know our neighbors about as well as we know the mail carrier—a smile, a wave, and we rush on our way.

---

7. Little, *How to Give Away Your Faith*, p. 131.

8. John Stott, as quoted by Paul E. Little in *How to Give Away Your Faith*, p. 130.

How can you extend your friendship to your unsaved neighbors?

_____

_____

_____

As you do, remember what they really want from you:

1. They want to see what's inside you—the real you.
2. They want to know that you are listening to them.
3. They want you to scratch them, spiritually speaking, where they itch.
4. They want you to talk *with them, not at them.*

What needs do your neighbors have to which you can minister?

_____

_____

How can you tactfully speak about your faith in Christ with them?

_____

_____

Chapter 18

PERSECUTOR BECOMES PREACHER

Acts 9:1–22

The life of Francis Thompson was a downward spiral that landed him on the streets of nineteenth-century London—a useless vagabond, an opium addict, a starving derelict. There, God caught him. Finally.

The son of a doctor, Thompson started out with great potential. His father sent him to study for the priesthood, and then to another school to become a doctor. But he failed at both professions and became a wastrel instead, running from responsibility, family, and God.

Eventually, this prodigal hit bottom. Wandering the back alleys of London, he was hungry, friendless, and addicted to drugs. With tattered clothes and broken shoes, he barely survived by selling matches and newspapers. Still, God did not relent in His dogged chase to capture the young man's soul.

A ray of hope came when Thompson began to write poetry. Wilfred Meynell, an editor, immediately saw Thompson's genius. He published his works, encouraged him to enter a hospital, and personally nursed him through his convalescence. This marked a spiritual turnaround in Thompson's life. He writes of his flight from God and God's pursuit of him in the poem "The Hound of Heaven."[1]

> I fled Him, down the nights and down the days;
> I fled Him, down the arches of the years;
> I fled Him, down the labyrinthine ways
> Of my own mind; and in the mist of tears
> I hid from Him, and under running laughter. . . .
> Still with unhurrying chase,
> And unperturbéd pace,
> Deliberate speed, majestic instancy,
> Came on the following Feet,
> And a Voice above their beat—

---

1. See *Cyclopedia of World Authors*, rev. ed., ed. Frank N. Magill (Englewood Cliffs, N.J.: Salem Press, 1974), p. 1762. Also, *Encyclopaedia Britannica*, 15th ed., see "Francis Thompson."

"Naught shelters thee, who wilt not shelter Me."[2]

With this same breathless pursuit, the Hound of Heaven once chased another running man. This person was not a vagrant; he was a well-educated Pharisee. Nonetheless, he stubbornly fled from Christ until, one day, the Hound caught him on the dusty road to Damascus.

Prior to Saul's Conversion

We know this man best as Paul, the great apostle. But he was first Saul of Tarsus, hater of Christ and scourge of Christianity. Luke wrote that Saul was in "hearty agreement" with the murder of Stephen (Acts 8:1a) and that he ravaged the church, "dragging off men and women" to torture and imprisonment (v. 3b, see also 26:10–11).

In spite of—even because of—his efforts, Christianity spread, as the apostles proclaimed the gospel in Samaria and Judea. But behind the scenes of these advances, Saul continued his vicious hunt.

> Saul, still breathing threats and murder against the disciples of the Lord, went to the high priest, and asked for letters from him to the synagogues at Damascus, so that if he found any belonging to the Way, both men and women, he might bring them bound to Jerusalem. (9:1–2)

Account of Saul's Conversion

Clutching the permission letters from the high priest, Saul sets out on his distorted mission. However, several days into the journey, the Hound of Heaven catches him and turns his world upside down.

Divine Phenomena

> It came about that as he journeyed, he was approaching Damascus, and suddenly a light from heaven flashed around him. (v. 3)

A light that shone brighter than the noonday sun stopped Saul as if he had run full speed into a wall (see also 26:12–13).

---

2. Francis Thompson, "The Hound of Heaven," in *A Treasury of the World's Best Loved Poems* (New York, N.Y.: Crown Publishers, Avenel Books, 1961), pp. 166–67.

And he fell to the ground, and heard a voice saying
to him, "Saul, Saul, why are you persecuting Me?"
(9:4)

At that moment, God captured Saul. The long chase had
climaxed—a climax Francis Thompson knew well:

Now of that long pursuit
Comes on at hand the bruit;
That Voice is round me like a bursting sea.[3]

Personal Dialogue

Saul answers the Voice's question with a question: "Who art
Thou, Lord?" (v. 5a).[4] He shows no remorse over persecuting Christians. At this point, his response is bewilderment: this light, this
voice—what could it . . . *who* could it be?

"I am Jesus whom you are persecuting" (v. 5b).

Saul's mind spins. Jesus? The Galilean, the blasphemer, the one
who died accursed and alone on a cross? *How can it be?*

The Voice continues, "Rise, and enter the city, and it shall be
told you what you must do" (v. 6).

As quickly as it had flashed, the light was gone. In seconds, like
the striking of a tornado, the Hound had come and gone. But for
those who were there, nothing would ever be the same.

The men who traveled with him stood speechless,
hearing the voice, but seeing no one. And Saul got
up from the ground, and though his eyes were open,
he could see nothing; and leading him by the hand,
they brought him into Damascus. (vv. 7–8)

Saul was at the bottom. This once-feared man, who had planned
to enter Damascus like a gripping north wind, now wisped quietly
into town, led by the hand.

Events after Saul's Conversion

As Saul enters Damascus, stumbling along blind, his inner eyes
begin to open. He has seen Jesus—alive and powerful. This one vi-

---

3. Thompson, "The Hound of Heaven," p. 170.

4. The word translated "Lord" is the Greek word *kurios*, which means "sir" in this context,
rather than "Lord God."

sion quakes his life's footing, and during this intense time, he neither eats nor drinks (v. 9).

Meanwhile, on the other side of town, another vision from God is shaking the life of a man named Ananias (v. 10).

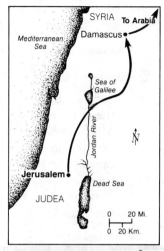

Saul Travels to Damascus[5]

A Vision: The Lord and Ananias

Ananias, like all the other Christians in Damascus, greatly fears the coming tempest of Saul's persecutions. But in his vision, God shocks him with this command:

> "Arise and go to the street called Straight, and inquire at the house of Judas for a man from Tarsus named Saul, for behold, he is praying, and he has seen in a vision a man named Ananias come in and lay his hands on him, so that he might regain his sight." (vv. 11–12)

Ananias knows nothing of Christ's appearance to Saul on the road. All he knows is Saul's cruel reputation. Fear floods his heart as he stutters back to the Lord,

> "Lord, I have heard from many about this man, how much harm he did to Thy saints at Jerusalem; and here he has authority from the chief priests to bind all who call upon Thy name." But the Lord said to him, "Go, for he is a chosen instrument of Mine, to bear My name before the Gentiles and kings and the sons of Israel; for I will show him how much he must suffer for My name's sake." (vv. 13b–16)

In Ananias' eyes, Saul was a murderer. In God's eyes, Saul was His chosen instrument. Like Ananias, we tend to view people the way they are, but God sees what they will become. He knew Saul's

5. *Life Application® Bible*, New International Version (copublishers; Wheaton, Ill.: Tyndale House Publishers, 1991 and Grand Rapids, Mich.: Zondervan Publishing House, 1991), p. 1964. Maps © 1986, 1988 by Tyndale House Publishers, Inc. All rights reserved. Used by permission.

potential and had already charted his life's course, including the persecution that he, the former persecutor, would endure.

A Contact: Ananias and Saul

Ananias obeys the Lord and goes to the house on Straight Street

> and after laying his hands on him said, "Brother Saul, the Lord Jesus, who appeared to you on the road by which you were coming, has sent me so that you may regain your sight, and be filled with the Holy Spirit." And immediately there fell from his eyes something like scales, and he regained his sight, and he arose and was baptized; and he took food and was strengthened. (vv. 17–19a)

With tenderness, Ananias ministers to undeserving Saul. As the blinding scales of hate fall away, Saul opens his eyes, and for the first time he sees the truth of Christ's love. And the two men embrace . . . once enemies, now brothers.

A Relationship: Saul and the Disciples

Since Saul had changed his view of Jesus, his educational goals needed to change, as well as his theological framework and his ambitions. His entire life philosophy needed reform. This renewal took place in the nurturing environment of the church.

"For several days," Luke records, "he was with the disciples who were at Damascus" (v. 19b). This is remarkable when one considers Saul's reputation. It was as if the Holocaust survivors had joined hands with the Gestapo officials. Only God's love can overcome such barriers of prejudice.

A Proclamation: Saul and Others

After being ministered to spiritually, Saul emerges proclaiming Christ. The persecutor has become the preacher.

> Immediately he began to proclaim Jesus in the synagogues, saying, "He is the Son of God." And all those hearing him continued to be amazed, and were saying, "Is this not he who in Jerusalem destroyed those who called on this name, and who had come here for the purpose of bringing them bound before the chief priests?" But Saul kept increasing in strength

and confounding the Jews who lived at Damascus by proving that this Jesus is the Christ. (vv. 20–22)

The Story Continues

The circumstances of Saul's transformation were unique, but the principles apply to us today. Christ still pursues, and we still run.

Are you running, sensing His footsteps but too proud or too afraid to let Him catch you? In the conclusion of "The Hound of Heaven," Francis Thompson finally surrendered when he heard Christ say:

> "Whom wilt thou find to love ignoble thee
>   Save Me, save only Me?
> All which I took from thee I did but take,
>   Not for thy harms,
> But just that thou might'st seek it in My arms.
>   All which thy child's mistake
> Fancies as lost, I have stored for thee at home:
>   Rise, clasp My hand, and come!"

>   Halts by me that footfall:
>   Is my gloom, after all,
>   Shade of His hand, outstretched caress-
>   ingly?
>   "Ah, fondest, blindest, weakest,
>   I am He Whom thou seekest!
>   Thou dravest love from thee, who dravest
>   Me."[6]

☼ Living Insights

In "The Hound of Heaven," Francis Thompson imagines God as the Divine Hunter—relentless, untiring, and trailing his every step. He fears what God will do if He catches him, so he runs, stumbling deeper into the darkness.

Are you running from God? Are you afraid of what God will do if He catches you? If so, write down some of your fears.

---

6. Thompson, "The Hound of Heaven," p. 170.

147

_____

_____

_____

By the end of Thompson's poem, his view of God has changed. He sees God as his Divine Lover—tender, caring, and healing his every wound. His fears melt in the warmth of God's love. The dreaded capture turns out to be his own salvation; God's mysterious shadow becomes his haven.

God pursues us our whole lives, but He can only capture us if we surrender to Him. Do you hesitate to let God capture you? Meditate on the following verses, and in prayer, surrender yourself to the Lord who loves you so much.

> O taste and see that the Lord is good;
> How blessed is the man who takes refuge in Him!
> (Ps. 34:8)

> Humble yourselves, therefore, under the mighty hand of God, that He may exalt you at the proper time, casting all your anxiety upon Him, because He cares for you. (1 Pet. 5:6–7)

☀ *Living Insights*   STUDY TWO

The Hound of Heaven pursues not only you, but those you love as well—your unbelieving spouse, your wayward brother, your lonely friend. You may have given up on them long ago, but the Hound perseveres in the chase. He has them in sight. He is right at their heels.

What drives our Lord to keep up His never-ending pursuit? See 1 Timothy 2:3–4 and 2 Peter 3:9.

_____

_____

Why does God continue chasing those we love even though they shun Him again and again? See Psalm 103:8–10.

148

Why is it so difficult for those we love to surrender to God? See John 3:19 and Romans 8:7.

How will God penetrate their defenses? See John 12:31–32 and 16:7–8.

What can we do to help them turn their lives over to Christ? See Romans 10:1; 1 Thessalonians 2:7–8; and 1 Peter 3:15–16.

Although your loved ones may seem to have drifted far from God, He is actually close at hand, closer than they realize. God captured Saul on the way to Damascus. He can catch your loved one anywhere, anytime.

Take a few moments right now to pray for your wandering loved one.

Chapter 19

A MAN WITHOUT AN IDENTITY

Acts 9:19–31

Whenn Saul put his lips to the cup of life that Christ offered, his thirsty soul yearned no more. At that moment, peace soothed his tortured mind. He had become a Christian, a follower of Jesus.

Saul's first few days following his conversion must have been rapturous. Many of us have experienced this phase as new believers. Having severed our worldly moorings, the Holy Spirit's tide washes us out onto a blissful sea. "The Christian life is easy," we say, as we bob along, soaking in the pleasures of God.

Then the lacy clouds darken and the seas begin to swell. In this second phase, disillusionment crashes like a thunderstorm. Troubles strike like lightning, and just holding on becomes our top priority. "This is difficult," we sputter, wiping the rain from our eyes.

Then we enter the third phase.

A hurricane of hardship blows our way, splintering our little boat, tossing us into the spewing sea. Flailing against doubt and despair, we wail, "This is impossible!"

If you have sailed into this third phase, you are not alone. Saul endured hurricanes too. We'll see him pass through all three phases—easy, difficult, and impossible. As we follow him, let's watch for principles that will help us keep afloat during our own tempestuous times.

The First Few Days: The Honeymoon Stage

For Saul, conversion to Christianity was dramatic. A sudden burst of light, a voice from heaven, blindness, and a miraculous healing highlighted the three days that forever changed his life. Equally exciting were his next few days as a new believer. Three factors contributed to his euphoria in this initial phase.

First, Saul enjoyed *close fellowship* with the believers in Damascus—the ones he had intended to persecute (Acts 9:19b). Fully accepted by them, Saul received affirmation and support. As a result, he felt secure enough to openly preach the gospel (v. 20).

This *open proclamation* was the second factor contributing to his joy as a new believer. Like many celebrities who convert to Christianity, Saul immediately stepped into the spotlight to give his testimony. Mouths dropped open as people crowded to hear him speak. Could this be Saul, the Christian-hater, proclaiming Jesus?

The third factor that eased his life as a new believer was the *public acclaim.* "All those hearing him continued to be amazed," Luke notes (v. 21a). The Greek verb translated "amazed" in this verse is the root for our word *ecstasy.*[1] They were ecstatic about his change of heart, and

> Saul kept increasing in strength and confounding the Jews who lived at Damascus by proving that this Jesus is the Christ. (v. 22)

The Following Months: Operation Obscurity

It did not take long for him to enter the second phase. What had been easy for Saul soon became difficult. Luke scarcely mentions this time, saying only, "when many days had elapsed" (v. 23a). From another passage, however, we learn that Saul experienced many growing pains during these days.

Hidden in Arabia

In his letter to the Galatians, Saul described this time:

> But when He who had set me apart, even from my mother's womb, and called me through His grace, was pleased to reveal His Son in me, that I might preach Him among the Gentiles, I did not immediately consult with flesh and blood, nor did I go up to Jerusalem to those who were apostles before me; but I went away to Arabia. (1:15–17a)

Arabia? What did he do there? Why did he go? How long was he there? We can only guess at the answers.[2] A cloak of obscurity covers this period in Saul's life—a cloak that may have initially smothered some of his enthusiasm.

1. The Greek verb *existēmi* is a combination of "out"—*ek*, and "to stand"—*histemi*. Literally, the word means "to be beside oneself."

2. Saul could have spent as long as three years in Arabia before returning to Damascus (Gal. 1:18).

Are you enduring an Arabian period, feeling lost and ineffective? Are you spinning your wheels, anxious to move on but going nowhere? This difficult time may last months or even years, but it will be invaluable. For in the desert, God teaches some of His best lessons.

Taught in Secret

S. D. Gordon emphasizes the importance of this desert learning experience for all of us:

> God is anxious that His children get a good education. . . . Every man He has used has had a course in the university of Arabia, a wilderness training. Joseph, Moses, Elijah, John the Herald, Paul . . . Morrison, Judson, even the divine Son Himself . . . these are a few of the distinguished graduates. But the fees are large, the course severely high, the discipline exacting, and many don't keep it up but drop out. The marked results are broad perspective, steady nerves, keen eyesight and insight. There come utter dependence on God, utter independence of man, childlike simplicity, warm sympathy and deep humility. But the highest degree goes to patience, the rarest trait of all, most God-like, hardest and longest to acquire. God has no short-cuts in His training.[3]

From a human perspective, Saul had an impressive resume. Though he was highly educated, in God's eyes Saul was completely useless until he graduated from God's Desert School of Character Development. If you're enrolled in that school right now, be encouraged. This is God's way of weaving steel into the fabric of your life.

Return to Activity: Reentry to Realism

Having matured in the desert, Saul "returned once more to Damascus" (Gal. 1:17b). In Acts 9:23b, Luke picks up Saul's story and continues through verse 31. Here the difficulties of the second phase give way to the challenging hardships of the next phase. "This

---

3. S. D. Gordon, as quoted by J. Oswald Sanders in *Robust in Faith* (Chicago, Ill.: Moody Press, 1965), p. 202.

is impossible," Saul may have thought, as he faced opposition from four groups of people.

The Damascus Jews

The first attack came in Damascus, where "the Jews plotted together to do away with him" (v. 23b). Luke reports that "they were also watching the gates day and night so that they might put him to death" (v. 24b). Their plot even included a high-ranking city official, as Saul recalls later.

> In Damascus the ethnarch under Aretas the king was guarding the city of the Damascenes in order to seize me. (2 Cor. 11:32)

For the first time, but not the last, Saul's life was threatened because of his beliefs. God intervened, though, and "their plot became known to Saul" (Acts 9:24a). So,

> his disciples took him by night, and let him down through an opening in the wall, lowering him in a large basket. (v. 25)

Imagine Saul's humiliation as he, who was once applauded by his peers, now becomes a common fugitive, escaping in a basket. Alone, rejected, and fearing for his life, Saul goes to Jerusalem for support. But he finds opposition there also, from an unexpected source.

The Jerusalem Disciples

The Christians in Jerusalem react differently to Saul than the Damascus believers.

> When he had come to Jerusalem, he was trying to associate with the disciples; and they were all afraid of him, not believing that he was a disciple. (v. 26)

When his new brothers and sisters in Christ shunned him, Saul's heart must have sunk. Had his grand conversion, his years of training, his courageous stand for Christ all come to this? Hated by his own people because he was a Christian, spurned by Christians because of his past, he was indeed a man without an identity.

> But Barnabas took hold of him and brought him to the apostles and described to them how he had seen

the Lord on the road, and that He had talked to him, and how at Damascus he had spoken out boldly in the name of Jesus. And he was with them moving about freely in Jerusalem, speaking out boldly in the name of the Lord. (vv. 27–28)

"But Barnabas took hold of him." This one phrase speaks volumes about the sensitivity of Barnabas. He was the only one who reached out to lonely Saul, stood by him, and made his impossible situation bearable.

Barnabas had the vision to see beyond Saul's past, to see his potential. He also had the courage to speak up for Saul, refusing to sway with the winds of public opinion. In addition, he showed determination. He gave no thought to his own reputation but unselfishly identified with the outcast.

Barnabas' ministry of encouragement continues to be one of the most needed in the family of God. Who can use that kind of encouragement? Those who have lost a job or failed in marriage or suffered rejection. These people need someone to come alongside, to hold them up and offer hope.

The Hellenistic Jews

Saul's hardships intensify when he collides with the same group of Jews who had stoned Stephen, the Hellenists—his former friends.

He was talking and arguing with the Hellenistic Jews; but they were attempting to put him to death. (v. 29)

Again Saul's life was in danger. Why did the Jews hate Saul? Donald Grey Barnhouse offers an insightful answer:

When truth has made a radical transformation in a life, there is only one thing we can do. We can admit that the power of God has been at work, and that, therefore, one's own life must be changed. The only other alternative is the one which Saul's enemies took: seek to destroy the evidence. Every martyrdom that has ever taken place has been an effort to destroy the evidence.[4]

4. Donald Grey Barnhouse with Herbert Henry Ehrenstein, *Acts: An Expositional Commentary* (Grand Rapids, Mich.: Zondervan Publishing House, Ministry Resources Library, 1979), p. 85.

So to protect Saul, the Jerusalem believers "brought him down to Caesarea and sent him away to Tarsus" (v. 30). They packed him up, shut him up, and pointed him back home. Surely Saul felt dejected as he boarded that ship for Tarsus. Was there no place for him?

The Church

In a subtle way, the believers in Jerusalem had communicated to Saul that they could do fine without him, thank you. In fact, Luke is quick to point out that after Saul left,

> the church throughout all Judea and Galilee and Samaria enjoyed peace, being built up; and, going on in the fear of the Lord and in the comfort of the Holy Spirit, it continued to increase. (v. 31)

Saul's Return to Tarsus[5]

Saul drops out of sight here in chapter 9 and doesn't reappear until chapter 11. Actually, years pass before Barnabas journeys to Tarsus to find Saul (11:25). The church had completely lost track of him.

What a disillusioning experience for Saul! It was all part of this third stage of Christian growth, when hardships make life seem impossible. It was during this time that Saul learned two principles from which we, too, can profit.

Application for Today

First, in our Christian growth, God does everything possible to stop the energy of the flesh. In Saul's early days of ministry, he may have been tempted to rely on himself. Likewise, when we depend on our own abilities rather than on the Spirit, God removes us to the desert or to a faraway Tarsus to teach us to trust Him alone. Don't chafe at His plan to curb your fleshly instincts; instead, learn what He is teaching you.

5. *Life Application® Bible*, New International Version (copublishers; Wheaton, Ill.: Tyndale House Publishers, 1991 and Grand Rapids, Mich.: Zondervan Publishing House, 1991), p. 1968. Maps © 1986, 1988 by Tyndale House Publishers, Inc. All rights reserved. Used by permission.

Second, in the world of ministry, no one but Christ is indispensable. Throughout Saul's life, the humility God forged on the anvil of failure safeguarded him against self-destructive pride. He had to discover humility in the lonely times—the times when he felt like a man without an identity.

If you feel cast aside like Saul, remember what eventually happened to him. He became Paul, Christ's flagship missionary who sailed the world with the gospel. What adventurous course has the Lord charted for your future? It is waiting for you, on the other side of the storm.

☼ *Living Insights*

Are you riding out a storm right now? Maybe you're enduring a difficult period in which you feel like Saul in Arabia—isolated, unproductive, waiting. Or perhaps you're in the midst of an impossible period like Saul had in Damascus and Jerusalem when he felt threatened, afraid, rejected.

If either of these experiences describe your situation, write down what is happening, as well as your feelings.

_____

_____

_____

_____

As waves of pressure crash around you, keep in mind the advice Hudson Taylor once offered. As an early missionary to inland China, he floundered through days of doubt and despair. But he knew a secret for staying afloat:

> It doesn't matter, really, how great the pressure is
> . . . it only matters *where the pressure lies*. See that
> it never comes *between* you and the Lord—then, the
> greater the pressure, the more it presses you to His
> breast.[6]

6. Dr. and Mrs. Howard Taylor, *Hudson Taylor's Spiritual Secret* (Chicago, Ill.: Moody Press, n.d.), p. 152.

Have you felt close to the Lord in the midst of your storm, or have you allowed the winds to force you away from Him?

____

____

____

If you've felt distant from Christ, what can you do in the days ahead to guard against the pressures that come between you and Him?

____

____

In what ways can the storm press you closer to Him?

____

____

____

What is He teaching you through these pressures?

____

____

____

Take a moment to thank the Lord for what you are learning during your storm, for they are lessons you will always treasure.

____

____

____

Living Insights STUDY TWO

"It is hard to be a Christian," admits Brennan Manning. "But," he adds, "it is too dull to be anything else."[7] Isn't that true? There is nothing more difficult yet more exciting than following Jesus.

Has Christianity lost its excitement for you? If so, maybe it's because you've stopped living by faith. Saul was constantly dangling out on faith's precipice, marveling at how God would never let him fall.

Evaluate your level of faith during a recent difficulty. Were you out on the edge, completely trusting Christ? Or were you clutching safety, anxiously relying on yourself?

_____

_____

Hudson Taylor knew how to live by faith. "I have just to roll the burden on the Lord," he would say.[8] While this simple faith is not easy, it is incredibly exhilarating.

Are you ready to roll your burden on the Lord? In the space provided, express your reckless faith in God concerning a present anxiety.

_____

_____

_____

_____

_____

_____

_____

7. Brennan Manning, *The Signature of Jesus* (Portland, Oreg.: Multnomah Press, 1992), p. 41.

8. Taylor, *Hudson Taylor's Spiritual Secret*, p. 209.

Chapter 20

SUPERNATURAL
MANIFESTATIONS

Acts 9:32–43

Lord, make my life a miracle."[1]

This prayer, voiced long ago by Thomas Kelly, is one God loves to answer. He savors turning our fear into courage and our hatred into love. He enjoys transforming us into new creations, evidences of His miraculous touch.

Scripture displays one life that is surely one of God's most gratifying exhibits—Peter, the fisherman Jesus reeled in one day on the shores of Galilee. Far from a miracle at first, Jesus' catch was rough-edged and sometimes self-centered. Peter was even prone to failure, for on the night of Jesus' arrest, he denied Him three times: "I do not know the man!" (Matt. 26:74b).

But God's grace searched him out in his darkness and sparked in him a miracle. In Acts, we've already seen the results of that miracle. It was Peter who preached at Pentecost, challenged the pompous Sanhedrin, and confronted church hypocrisy. Now in chapter 9, as Luke closes the account of Saul's conversion, Peter once again showed his changed heart. In this passage, Luke reveals just how miraculous Peter's life had become. For now, with the Spirit's power, he was the one performing the miracles.

Great Eras of Miracles

Peter's miracles occurred during one of the great eras of miracles in the Bible. In these eras, supernatural manifestations were more frequent because God was validating the authority of certain people to perform special tasks. Apart from these periods, miracles are actually rare in Scripture. The following chart outlines the three eras of miracles and includes God's purposes for His miracles at these times.

1. Thomas Kelly, as quoted by Raymond C. Ortlund in *Lord, Make My Life a Miracle!* (Glendale, Calif.: G/L Publications, Regal Books, 1974), p. 2.

Moses	Elijah and Elisha	Christ and the Apostles
To establish God's authority	To give testimony to Israel	To fulfill scriptural prophecies
To authenticate Moses as God's servant	To awaken the nation in the midst of apostasy	To validate the message and character of Christ and the apostles

Today, God does not work miracles through us like He did through Moses, the prophets, Jesus, or the apostles. Instead, we have something previously unavailable to help us discern whether God's presence validates a ministry—we have the finished Word of God. John Walvoord addresses this in his book *The Holy Spirit*.

> With the completion of the New Testament, . . . the need for further unusual display of miraculous works ceased. The preacher of today does not need the outward evidence of ability to heal . . . to substantiate the validity of his gospel. Rather, the written Word speaks for itself, and is attended by the convicting power of the Spirit.[2]

We are not saying, of course, that God does not perform miracles today. "It is not a question of the power of God to perform miracles," Walvoord explains,

> but simply whether it is His purpose to continue the same form of manifestation of divine power as seen in the apostolic times.[3]

There is no question, however, that it is His purpose to continue miracles of the heart. These inner spiritual miracles cross all eras and are truly the most impressive (see Mark 2:9–11). God worked one in Peter's life, and through his ministry worked thousands more in the lives of others.

2. John F. Walvoord, *The Holy Spirit* (Grand Rapids, Mich.: Zondervan Publishing House, Academic and Professional Books, 1991), p. 174.

3. Walvoord, *The Holy Spirit*, p. 174.

Two Accounts of Miracles

Let's accompany Peter on his visits to two cities and observe God's amazing power shown through him. On these visits, let's ask ourselves: What can we learn about God's miracles in our lives? And what can we learn about the practices of ministers who claim to be miracle workers today?

The Man at Lydda: The Case of Aeneas

Picking up the story line from Acts 8:25, where Peter and John had been returning from Samaria to Jerusalem "preaching the gospel to many villages of the Samaritans," Luke writes:

> Now it came about that as Peter was traveling through all those parts, he came down also to the saints who lived at Lydda. And there he found a certain man named Aeneas, who had been bedridden eight years, for he was paralyzed. (9:32–33)

What caused his paralysis? Did he fall? Did he have a disease? Luke does not give us these details. He only mentions that for eight years Aeneas had been confined to bed.

Only a victim of paralysis can truly understand Aeneas' inner agony. One such victim is Joni Eareckson Tada. Since 1967, she has been paralyzed from the neck down as the result of a diving accident. She knows what it is like to hear the words, "You will never walk again." She understands the frustrations, the self-hatred, the helplessness, and the anger that must have tormented Aeneas.

When Peter came to him, he saw all these emotions and compassionately said,

> "Aeneas, Jesus Christ heals you; arise, and make your bed." (v. 34a)

Then Luke adds simply: "And immediately he arose" (v. 34b).

Amazing! With a simple command, Aeneas' severed nerves joined, his legs tingled once more with feeling, and his atrophied muscles awakened from their deep sleep. He stretched for a moment and then stood for the first time in eight years!

> And all who lived at Lydda and Sharon saw him, and they turned to the Lord. (v. 35)

Through this miracle, a spiritual awakening spread throughout the region.

For a moment, let's step back from the story to observe Peter's method of healing compared to that of modern faith healers. First, we notice that Peter found Aeneas—Aeneas did not have to come to Peter or to a meeting for his healing. Second, there was no large gathering or big spectacle; no hysteria or hype. Third, the healing was immediate and complete; the result of one simple sentence. Fourth, Jesus was the focus. Peter made it clear that "Jesus Christ heals you," and the people who heard about the miracle "turned to the Lord," not to Peter.

Restoring strength to the legs of a paralytic is incredible, but God's healing power is even greater than that. Let's return to Peter's story and notice what happens next.

The Woman at Joppa: The Case of Tabitha

About ten miles away, in the city of Joppa, there lived a woman named Tabitha, whose Greek name was Dorcas.

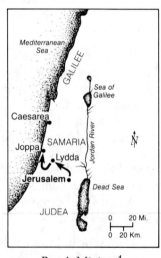

Peter's Ministry[4]

> This woman was abounding with deeds of kindness and charity, which she continually did. And it came about at that time that she fell sick and died; and when they had washed her body, they laid it in an upper room. (vv. 36b–37)

Tabitha's death stunned the Christian community in Joppa, where she was adored for her sweet, giving spirit.

> Since Lydda was near Joppa, the disciples, having heard that Peter was there, sent two men to him, entreating him, "Do not delay to come to us." And Peter arose and went with them. And when he had

4. *Life Application® Bible*, New International Version (copublishers; Wheaton, Ill.: Tyndale House Publishers, 1991 and Grand Rapids, Mich.: Zondervan Publishing House, 1991), p. 1969. Maps © 1986, 1988 by Tyndale House Publishers, Inc. All rights reserved. Used by permission.

come, they brought him into the upper room; and all the widows stood beside him weeping, and showing all the tunics and garments that Dorcas used to make while she was with them. But Peter sent them all out and knelt down and prayed, and turning to the body, he said, "Tabitha, arise." And she opened her eyes, and when she saw Peter, she sat up. And he gave her his hand and raised her up; and calling the saints and widows, he presented her alive. (vv. 38–41)

Through Peter, God restored life to the dead woman. This miracle is remarkably similar to an event in Jesus' life. Jesus had come to the house of Jairus, whose daughter had just died. Mourners wept and wailed, but Jesus calmly took control. He asked everyone to leave the house and took a few people, including Peter, into the girl's room to witness what He was about to do.

And taking the child by the hand, He said to her, "Talitha kum!" (which translated means, "Little girl, I say to you, arise!") And immediately the girl rose and began to walk. (Mark 5:41–42a)

This miracle must have etched an indelible mark in Peter's mind, for he closely emulated Jesus' words and actions in Tabitha's healing.

The results of this second miracle were the same as in Lydda: the news spread and "many believed in the Lord" (Acts 9:42). Luke then concludes the story by telling us that Peter remained in Joppa, staying with a tanner named Simon (v. 43).

Peter's life certainly fulfilled Jesus' previous promise:

Truly, truly, I say to you, he who believes in Me, the works that I do shall he do also; and greater works than these shall he do; because I go to the Father. (John 14:12)

Some Comments and Conclusions about Miracles

Just as Jesus' miracles impacted Peter, so Peter's miracles affect us, causing us to review the two questions posed earlier. First, what can we learn about God's miracles in our lives?

These two vignettes from Peter's ministry remind us that *not all of God's miracles are physical.* Many of God's miracles cure spiritual diseases that involve emotional paralysis.

If God were to examine your life, would He notice an unresponsive heart, an inability to enjoy life, an inner numbness? Would He see death inside you—the death of the love you once had for your spouse or for a friend, the death of hope, the death of joy?

God can miraculously revive your heart's emotions. He can restore your faith and give you purpose. He *can* make your life a miracle.

Second, what can we learn about the practices of ministers who claim to be miracle workers today? Peter's example teaches us that *when the miracle is of God, a consistent pattern occurs.* That pattern includes the following elements:

1. The Lord alone is glorified.
2. There is no showmanship, only integrity and authenticity.
3. The unsaved are impressed and often trust Christ for salvation.
4. Biblical principles are never contradicted.

God does heal physical diseases today. But He always performs these miracles on His own terms. Joni writes out of her own experience:

> God certainly can, and sometimes does, heal people in a miraculous way today. But the Bible does *not* teach that He will *always* heal those who come to Him in faith. He sovereignly reserves the right to heal or not to heal as He sees fit.[5]

Be wary of those who stage high-powered healing spectacles and claim that God always heals those who have faith. From Peter's example, that is not God's way. It is God's way, though, to bring spiritual healing to our souls. Christ's words are true and His invitation is still open:

> Whoever drinks of the water that I shall give him shall never thirst; but the water that I shall give him shall become in him a well of water springing up to eternal life. (John 4:14)

Now that's miraculous!

5. Joni Eareckson and Steve Estes, *A Step Further* (Grand Rapids, Mich.: Zondervan Publishing House, 1978), p. 127.

Take a little time right now to examine your own heart for signs of emotional paralysis. Use the following checklist to mark any symptoms that apply to your condition.

❏ sleeplessness	❏ anxiety
❏ absence of laughter	❏ lethargy
❏ indifference toward others	❏ self-doubt
❏ emotional numbness	❏ lack of faith

Now what's your diagnosis? What do you think is the cause of your symptoms? Do you see any bitterness or resentment, fear or anger?

_____

_____

_____

God's healing process can turn your life into a miracle. What prescription do you think He is giving you now? Do you need to forgive someone? Resolve an argument? Revitalize your spiritual life? Write down what He is telling you to do.

_____

_____

_____

_____

At some point in our lives, many of us will grapple with the question, "If God loves me, why doesn't He heal me?" Joni Eareckson Tada has wrestled with this question like few others, when once she was convinced God would heal her. She tells the story:

On a rainy afternoon in the early summer of 1972

about fifteen people gathered together in a tiny oak church not far from my home. The group consisted of close friends, family, and church leaders . . . whom I had called together to pray for my healing.
. . .

    By the time our brief service was over, the rain had stopped. Exiting through the front doors of the church, we were greeted by a beautiful rainbow in the misty distance. . . . It gave me just one more reassurance that God was looking down on us right there and had heard our prayers.[6]

God did hear Joni's prayers, but He still didn't heal her. Some might say the healing failed because she had hidden sin or her method was wrong or she lacked faith. She evaluated each of these reasons in her heart, however, and concluded, "The answer must lie elsewhere."[7]

She found the answer in several Scripture passages that helped her better understand the nature of God and sin.[8] One passage was Romans 8:18–25. Take the time to read it now.

How has sin affected creation and us (vv. 20, 22–23)?

_____

_____

God has a plan to free creation and us from these destructive effects. What does His plan offer (vv. 18–19, 21, 23)?

_____

_____

Jesus initiated this plan. What is the evidence in our hearts that His plan has started (v. 23)?

_____

_____

6. Eareckson and Estes, A Step Further, pp. 122–23.

7. Eareckson and Estes, A Step Further, pp. 124–26.

8. For a complete understanding of Joni's position on healing, read A Step Further, pp. 115–58.

Since God is in the process of freeing us from the effects of sin, how are we to respond to suffering (vv. 24–25)?

_____

_____

God does love us—that's why He has a plan to one day completely free us from all the effects of sin, including disease. Why doesn't He heal us right now? Only He knows that answer. The question is, Will I trust Him during the wait?

BOOKS FOR PROBING FURTHER

Long ago, Christ told a handful of people, "You shall be My witnesses . . . to the remotest part of the earth" (Acts 1:8b), and He continues to say that to us today. For some, telling every person on our planet about Christ seems impossible—a fool's errand, like Don Quixote attacking a windmill. But we serve a God who delights in doing the impossible.

In this study, we've witnessed the birth of His impossible vision. We have watched it endure birth pangs of persecution and grow through infancy. And as we continue to explore the book of Acts in the next two study guides in this series, we'll see the church stretch and mature even more.

No, we're not Don Quixotes, mistaking windmills for giants and dreams for reality. The world *can* know Jesus; we just need to catch the vision.

To help you become personally involved in Christ's vision for the world, we suggest the following books as helpful guides. Remember, Acts is an unfinished book—it is still being written by all of us. We hope that the following books will help you write your own chapter of the Acts story.

Missions

Borthwick, Paul. A *Mind for Missions*. Colorado Springs, Colo.: Navpress, 1987. This book will launch you on a lifetime journey of missions involvement. Even if you are not called to be a foreign missionary, Borthwick shows you how to involve yourself and your family in world missions.

Hawthorne, Steve, ed. *Stepping Out: A Guide to Short-Term Missions*. Evanston, Ill.: Berry Publishing Services, 1987. This book outlines everything you need to become involved with a short-term mission project. It includes helpful articles on every aspect of short-term missions and a complete address list of mission agencies you can write for information. A more thorough handbook on this subject is hard to find. For ordering information, write to Berry Publishing Services, 701 Main, Evanston, Illinois 60202.

Commentaries on the Book of Acts

Barnhouse, Donald Grey. *Acts: An Expositional Commentary.* Grand Rapids, Mich.: Zondervan Publishing House, Ministry Resources Library, 1979. In this treatment of Acts, Barnhouse uses his preaching and expositional skills to make the book come alive. His illustrations and insights will help you both learn and apply the truth.

Bruce, F. F. *Commentary on the Book of the Acts.* Grand Rapids, Mich.: William B. Eerdmans Publishing Co., 1970. Bruce's scholarly research on Acts is unparalleled. He presents his material in a readable, delightful, informative fashion that will help anyone better understand Acts.

Suffering for Christ

Brown, Joan Winmill, ed. *Dietrich Bonhoeffer: The Martyred Christian.* New York, N.Y.: Macmillan Publishing Co., Collier Books, 1983. This compilation of some of Dietrich Bonhoeffer's writings will challenge you with his commitment to Christ. A twentieth-century Stephen, Bonhoeffer died while condemning the powerful Nazi war machine. His life is a model of Christian courage.

White, John. *Magnificent Obsession: The Joy of Christian Commitment.* Revised edition. Downers Grove, Ill.: InterVarsity Press, 1990. Not all suffering is suffering for Christ. White explains the different types of suffering and leads you to commit yourself to the Lord, no matter what the cost.

Yancey, Philip. *Where Is God When It Hurts?* Grand Rapids, Mich.: Zondervan Publishing House, 1990. Keith Miller's recommendation for this book says it all: "I've read everything I can get my hands on about the problems of pain and evil, and this book is the clearest, most practical thing I've read."

The Church

Aldrich, Joseph C. *Gentle Persuasion.* Portland, Oreg.: Multnomah Press, 1988. The subtitle of this book is "Creative Ways to Introduce Your Friends to Christ." Aldrich offers a wealth of ideas to help you make connections with your unsaved neighbors. You can spread the flame of Christ in your own hometown, one friend at a time.

Colson, Charles, with Ellen Santilli Vaughn. *Against the Night*. Ann Arbor, Mich.: Servant Publications, Vine Books, 1989. According to Colson and Vaughn, we are living in the new dark ages, a time when barbarian ethics are on the rise. Can the church make a difference? Only if we are willing to really live out the kingdom principles of Christ—just like the early church did.

Schaller, Lyle E. *Looking in the Mirror: Self-Appraisal in the Local Church*. Nashville, Tenn.: Abington Press, 1984. This book helps leaders measure the ministry potential of their churches. From youth ministries to the nursery program, Schaller guides churches to become more like the New Testament model.

Miracles

Barron, Bruce. *The Health and Wealth Gospel*. Downers Grove, Ill.: InterVarsity Press, 1987. With chapter titles that pose pointed questions, such as "Does God Want You Healthy?" and "Does the Bible Really Say That?", the author evaluates the popular "name it, claim it" theology of some charismatic teachers.

Eareckson, Joni, and Steve Estes. *A Step Further*. Grand Rapids, Mich.: Zondervan Publishing House, 1978. This book was written in response to the thousands of letters Joni had received about healing and miracles. With warmth and understanding, the authors focus on understanding God's perspective on pain and physical limitations.

Some of the books listed here may be out of print and available only through a library. All of these works are recommended reading only. With the exception of books by Charles R. Swindoll, none of them are available through Insight for Living. If you wish to obtain some of these suggested readings, please contact your local Christian bookstore.

ORDERING INFORMATION

Cassette Tapes and Study Guide

This Bible study guide was designed to be used independently or in conjunction with the broadcast of Chuck Swindoll's taped messages on the topic listed below. If you would like to order cassette tapes or further copies of this study guide, please see the information given below and the Order Forms provided at the end of this guide

THE BIRTH OF AN EXCITING VISION

Did you know that Acts is the only unfinished book of the Bible? Powerfully begun with Christ's ascension and the Holy Spirit's arrival at Pentecost, it traces the story of the church's birth and growth . . . and waits for our stories to make the book complete. It is the dramatic account of Christ's spreading flame—first to Jerusalem, next to Judea and Samaria, then ultimately reaching to the remotest regions of place and time.

In this study of the first few chapters of Acts, we'll witness the lighting of this flame and see it passed on to the first few torchbearers. Join us, won't you? Let's share in the birth of this exciting vision!

			Calif.*	U.S.	B.C.*	Canada*
BEV	CS	Cassette series, includes album cover	$73.47	$68.50	$84.00	$79.80
BEV	1–10	Individual cassettes, includes messages A and B	6.76	6.30	7.61	7.23
BEV	SG	Study guide	5.31	4.95	6.37	6.37

*These prices already include the following charges: for delivery in **California**, applicable sales tax; Canada, 7% GST and 7% postage and handling (on tapes only); **British Columbia**, 7% GST, 6% British Columbia sales tax (on tapes only), and 7% postage and handling (on tapes only). **The prices are subject to change without notice.**

BEV   1-A: *The Spreading Flame*—Survey of Acts
      B: *Operation Revolution*—Acts 1:1–14

BEV   2-A: *Dice in the Prayer Meeting*—Acts 1:12–26
      B: *Supernatural Churchbirth*—Acts 2:1–13

BEV   3-A: *Peter's First Sermon . . . and Best*—Acts 2:12–31
      B: *The Birth of 3,000 Babies*—Acts 2:37–41

BEV 4-A: *Spiritual Pediatrics*—Acts 2:41–47
          B: *The Cripple Who Danced in Church*—Acts 3:1–26

BEV 5-A: *Religion versus Christianity*—Acts 4:1–22
          B: *Tough Without, Tender Within*—Acts 4:23–35

BEV 6-A: *A Deadly Game*—Acts 4:36–5:11
          B: *We Overwhelmingly Conquer*—Acts 5:12–42

BEV 7-A: *Operation Iceberg*—Acts 6:1–7
          B: *A Wise Man under Pressure*—Acts 6:8–15

BEV 8-A: *A Courageous Swan Song*—Acts 7
          B: *The Pure and the Phony*—Acts 8:1–24

BEV 9-A: *God's Way of Winning*—Acts 8:25–40
          B: *Persecutor Becomes Preacher*—Acts 9:1–22

BEV 10-A: *A Man without an Identity*—Acts 9:19–31
          B: *Supernatural Manifestations*—Acts 9:32–43

How to Order by Mail

Simply mark on the order form whether you want the series or individual tapes. Mail the form with your payment to the appropriate address listed below. We will process your order as promptly as we can.

United States: Mail your order to the Listener Services Department at Insight for Living, Post Office Box 69000, Anaheim, California 92817-0900. If you wish your order to be shipped first-class for faster delivery, add 10 percent of the total order amount. Otherwise, please allow four to six weeks for delivery by fourth-class mail. We accept payment by personal check, money order, or credit card. Unfortunately, we are unable to offer invoicing or COD orders.

Canada: Mail your order to Insight for Living Ministries, Post Office Box 2510, Vancouver, British Columbia V6B 3W7. Allow approximately four weeks for delivery. We accept payment by personal check, money order, or credit card. Unfortunately, we are unable to offer invoicing or COD orders.

Australia, New Zealand, or Papua New Guinea: Mail your order to Insight for Living, Inc., GPO Box 2823 EE, Melbourne, Victoria 3001, Australia. Please allow six to ten weeks for delivery by surface mail. If you would like your order sent airmail, the delivery time may be reduced. Using the United States price as a base, add postage costs—surface or airmail—to the amount of your order. Please use the chart that follows to determine correct postage. Due to fluctuating currency rates, we can accept only personal checks made payable in U.S. funds, international money orders, or credit cards in payment for materials.

Overseas: Other overseas residents should mail their orders to our United States office. Please allow six to ten weeks for delivery by surface mail. If you would like your order sent airmail, the delivery time may be reduced. Using the United States price as a base, add postage costs — surface or airmail — to the amount of your order. Please use the chart that follows to determine correct postage. Due to fluctuating currency rates, we can accept only personal checks made payable in U.S. funds, international money orders, or credit cards in payment for materials.

Type of Postage	Postage Cost
Surface	10% of total order
Airmail	25% of total order

For Faster Service, Order by Telephone or FAX

For credit card orders, you are welcome to use one of our toll-free numbers between the hours of 7:00 A.M. and 4:30 P.M., Pacific time, Monday through Friday, or our FAX numbers. The numbers to use from anywhere in the United States are **1-800-772-8888** or FAX (714) 575-5049. To order from Canada, call our Vancouver office using **1-800-663-7639** or FAX (604) 596-2975. Vancouver residents, call (604) 596-2910. Australian residents should phone (03) 872-4606. From other international locations, call our Listener Services Department at (714) 575-5000 in the United States.

Our Guarantee

Our cassettes are guaranteed for ninety days against faulty performance or breakage due to a defect in the tape. For best results, please be sure your tape recorder is in good operating condition and is cleaned regularly.

Note: To cover processing and handling, there is a $10 fee for *any* returned check.

Insight for Living Catalog

Request a free copy of the Insight for Living catalog of books, tapes, and study guides by calling **1-800-772-8888** in the United States or **1-800-663-7639** in Canada.

Order Form

BEV CS represents the entire *The Birth of an Exciting Vision* series in a special album cover, while BEV 1–10 are the individual tapes included in the series. BEV SG represents this study guide, should you desire to order additional copies.

Item	Unit Price Calif.*	U.S.	B.C.*	Canada*	Quantity	Amount
BEV CS	$73.47	$68.50	$84.00	$79.80		$
BEV 1	6.76	6.30	7.61	7.23		
BEV 2	6.76	6.30	7.61	7.23		
BEV 3	6.76	6.30	7.61	7.23		
BEV 4	6.76	6.30	7.61	7.23		
BEV 5	6.76	6.30	7.61	7.23		
BEV 6	6.76	6.30	7.61	7.23		
BEV 7	6.76	6.30	7.61	7.23		
BEV 8	6.76	6.30	7.61	7.23		
BEV 9	6.76	6.30	7.61	7.23		
BEV 10	6.76	6.30	7.61	7.23		
BEV SG	5.31	4.95	6.37	6.37		
					Subtotal	
	Overseas Residents *Pay U.S. price plus 10% surface postage or 25% airmail. Also, see "How to Order by Mail."*					
	U.S. First-Class Shipping *For faster delivery, add 10% for postage and handling.*					
	Gift to Insight for Living *Tax-deductible in the United States and Canada.*					
	Total Amount Due *Please do not send cash.*					$

If there is a balance: ❏ Apply it as a donation ❏ Please refund
*These prices already include applicable taxes and shipping costs.

Payment by: ❏ Check or money order payable to Insight for Living ❏ Credit card

(Circle one): Visa MasterCard Discover Card Number_____

Expiration Date_____ Signature_____

We cannot process your credit card purchase without your signature.

Name_____

Address_____

City_____ State/Province_____

Zip/Postal Code_____ Country_____

Telephone (___)_____ Radio Station___ ___ ___ ___

If questions arise concerning your order, we may need to contact you.

Mail this order form to the Listener Services Department at one of these addresses:
Insight for Living, Post Office Box 69000, Anaheim, CA 90017-0900
Insight for Living Ministries, Post Office Box 2510, Vancouver, BC, Canada V6B 3W7
Insight for Living, Inc., GPO Box 2823 EE, Melbourne, VIC 3001, Australia

Order Form

BEV CS represents the entire *The Birth of an Exciting Vision* series in a special album cover, while BEV 1–10 are the individual tapes included in the series. BEV SG represents this study guide, should you desire to order additional copies.

Item	Calif.*	Unit Price U.S.	B.C.*	Canada*	Quantity	Amount
BEV CS	$73.47	$68.50	$84.00	$79.80		$
BEV 1	6.76	6.30	7.61	7.23		
BEV 2	6.76	6.30	7.61	7.23		
BEV 3	6.76	6.30	7.61	7.23		
BEV 4	6.76	6.30	7.61	7.23		
BEV 5	6.76	6.30	7.61	7.23		
BEV 6	6.76	6.30	7.61	7.23		
BEV 7	6.76	6.30	7.61	7.23		
BEV 8	6.76	6.30	7.61	7.23		
BEV 9	6.76	6.30	7.61	7.23		
BEV 10	6.76	6.30	7.61	7.23		
BEV SG	5.31	4.95	6.37	6.37		
					Subtotal	
					Overseas Residents *Pay U.S. price plus 10% surface postage or 25% airmail. Also, see "How to Order by Mail."*	
					U.S. First-Class Shipping *For faster delivery, add 10% for postage and handling.*	
					Gift to Insight for Living *Tax-deductible in the United States and Canada.*	
					Total Amount Due *Please do not send cash.*	$

If there is a balance: ❑ Apply it as a donation ❑ Please refund
*These prices already include applicable taxes and shipping costs.

Payment by: ❑ Check or money order payable to Insight for Living ❑ Credit card

(Circle one): Visa MasterCard Discover Card Number_____

Expiration Date_____ Signature_____

We cannot process your credit card purchase without your signature.

Name_____

Address_____

City_____ State/Province_____

Zip/Postal Code_____ Country_____

Telephone (___)_____ Radio Station____ ____ ____ ____

If questions arise concerning your order, we may need to contact you.

Mail this order form to the Listener Services Department at one of these addresses:
Insight for Living, Post Office Box 69000, Anaheim, CA 92817-0300
Insight for Living Ministries, Post Office Box 2510, Vancouver, BC, Canada V6B 3W7
Insight for Living, Inc., GPO Box 2823 EE, Melbourne, VIC 3001, Australia